For Claire
Best wishes

Clive

Clive Nichols
New Shoots

Commentary by Lance Hattatt

NS

For Jane, Hazel and Robert

First published in the UK in 2000 by
New Shoots Ltd
69 Albert Road
Reading
Berkshire RG4 7AW
www.newshoots.com

Distributed in the UK by Fountain Press Ltd
Fountain House
2 Gladstone Road
Kingston-upon-Thames
Surrey KT1 3HD

British Library Cataloguing-in-Publication data

A catalogue record for this book is available from the British Library

ISBN 0-9538318-0-9

Edited by Joanna Smith
Designed by Clive Nichols and Joanna Smith
Production by Supreme Publishing Services, London
Printed in China

9 8 7 6 5 4 3 2 1

Picture captions:
p1 Butter Churn – yellow ranunculus
p2–3 Sweet Valentine – centre of red rose
p4–5 Moody Blues – blue hyacinth
p6–7 Finale – orange dahlia
p8–9 Larch Wood – *Melianthus major*
p10–11 Coxcomb – *Dahlia* 'David Howard'

C O N T E N T S

Introduction *14*

COLOUR *20*

PATTERN *48*

FORM *80*

LIGHT *110*

TEXTURE *138*

Directory *172*

New Shoots is an expression of artistic intent. It is the result of a creative imagination in which image triumphs over illustration. It is exploratory in content, inviting responses designed to unlock the deepest of all human emotions. It is a portrayal of the richness of an element of our world whose purpose is to open our minds to analysis and debate. To this end New Shoots is more than a series of technically perfected images recorded by the camera. It is the interpretation of these images by the eye of the photographer that is of interest. For in New Shoots Clive Nichols sets new standards of excellence, seeking to metamorphose contemporary studies of flower and foliage into exacting symbols which, in arresting our attention, are demanding of our intellect.

Nichols' work belongs to a long history of the aesthetics of photography, dating back to the first years of the twentieth century. As early as 1917 Alfred Stieglitz was able to write of Paul Strand: 'His work is rooted in the best tradition of photography... In whatever he does there is applied intelligence.' The same may be said of Nichols whose concern is primarily with the arrangement of form and colour within the context of an aesthetically pleasing composition rather than the reproduction of a recognisable subject. Indeed, complementary and contrasting colours, favouring strong, sometimes discordant tones, are used with an unerring confidence to emphasise the juxtaposition of, say, an individual flower against its surroundings. A control over depth of field enables Nichols to provide on the one hand bitingly sharp images latent with texture, on the other abstract compositions inspired by painters such as Howard Hodgkin and Mark Rothko.

As a garden and plant photographer, studio portraits or simulations hold no interest for Nichols who perceives such pictures as lifeless and contrived. Shunning the use of flash and rejecting filters, the vitality of his work is a direct result of his use of natural light, for which he believes there is no substitute. Variable light levels, combined with the unpredictability of a constantly changing subject matter, are for Nichols a challenge to be embraced. His acute awareness of the importance of light, and with it the necessity for perfection in the reproduction of his pictures, owes much to the influence of landscape photographers such as the Americans Ansel Adams, Tom Till, Elliot Porter and David Muench, as well as the master of black and white plant photography, the German Karl Blossfeldt.

The underlying philosophy of Nichols' work is as straightforward as it is undiluted. Simplicity is the key note with a concentration of emphasis on paring, reduction and omission in the belief that what is removed is as important as what remains. His creativity, that which raises his work to an art form, stems from his ability to go beyond what he sees through the lens. Denied this faculty his pictures, however competent, would do no more than become a factual record, an illustration of plant life. Recognition of the potentialities of the medium, an intensity of vision, heightened appreciation of objectivity, as well as mastery of the technical aspects of photography, are what give these images a startling uniqueness.

In *New Shoots*, Clive Nichols isolates areas of curiosity in the exploration and development of such themes as colour, texture, form, light and pattern to create a series of sequenced images which not only express the dispassionate view of the artist but allow for personal and individual interpretations. In so doing they permit us a revelation, to perceive familiar objects in a new and wondrous light as if seen for the first time. Such is the potency of the images. Our prejudices are swept aside, our preconceptions removed, our minds set free.

Colour is fundamental to Nichols' work. A passion. Strong tones, often daring, occasionally shocking, dominate. Painterly influence is seldom far away. Iris, poppy and tulip neatly ally themselves to the paintings of Hitchens, Picasso and Smith. In 'Porcelain Factory' the upturned heads of *Crocus* 'Remembrance' await the brush for final decoration. They belong as much to the production line of the potteries of Worcester as they do to the spring border. *Tulipa* 'Fantasy', titled 'Sixties Shades', returns us in time, a symbol of an age rapidly reaching into history. Here is the swinging London of Carnaby Street, the Beatles, a government led by Harold Wilson. A single flower captures a fantasy world, whose loss is mourned by a generation too young to remember.

Inherent in all the images presented here is a textural quality which allows the imagination to play. Tree bark is a recurring theme whether of *Prunus serrula*, suggestive of 'Punctured Plastic', or *Pinus nigra maritima*, 'Shale Stratum'. In contrast 'Liberty Print', *Cephalocereus senilis*, is central to the Art and Craft Movement, at its peak from around 1880 up to the Great War. Accepted as the major figure of the time, William Morris lives on for his designs, not least for wallpapers, carpets, textile and tapestries. Nichols' image could be one such.

The shape of an object remains of paramount importance to Nichols for it is his fascination for detail that is evident in so much of his work. Stripping away all that may be considered superfluous, he disciplines himself to concentrate on the essential. As observers, we may imagine and interpret what remains. Unconsciously we transfigure plants, shrubs and trees, even vegetables, into objects as far apart in time and space as a 'Turbo Jet' and a 'Furled Parasol'.

Hardy, in his novel *Tess of the D'Urbervilles*, comments on the effect of light 'leaving absolute mental liberty'. Nichols is at one with this. His images, whether of grand statues at Chiswick House, London, or of a single frosted rose, do exactly that. The mind is released from all constraints. None of this comes about by chance, as is apparent in 'How Green Was My Valley' where we witness the immediacy of the dawn breaking over a rural landscape in mid Wales. Similarly 'Cold Charmian' conveys the icy white light of a chilling January.

Pattern is integral to so much of Nichols' chosen subject matter. It is evident in the construction of the individual flower, in leaf, on bark, in whole gardens. It too becomes a preoccupation, something to be exploited, manipulated to an artistic end. At times it is construed as deeply serious, 'Ghostly Convoy', on occasion thought provoking, 'Inca Empire' or 'Stargazer', while often it invites humour as in 'Ice-capped Maidens' and 'Body Piercing'.

At the start of a new millennium the world appears to move away from nature. As more and more people come to inhabit our towns and cities, so that essential communion that once existed between man and his environment is lost. The landscape, with its many constituent parts, tamed or otherwise, that awakens our deepest responses seems to ebb away beyond our reach. That which impels all thinking is in retreat. Life takes on an artificial quality, existence becomes counterfeit. Fewer and fewer people tread real soil, walk bare foot in the grass, experience plants out of pots, delight in a star-spangled sky. An argument exists that, in reality, *New Shoots* can never be more than a remarkable collection of outstanding photographs, the record of a creative and sensitive individual with a vision to share. The pages that follow are a strong denial of this. For here, in a hundred or more images, is an enduring, silent testimony to the intimate link that we may still yet find and make with a world which, for the present, remains our own.

COLOUR

Strictly speaking, colour is no more than the sensation produced in the eye by rays of decomposed light. It comprises any one, or indeed any mixture, of the constituents into which light breaks down. What is perceived is entirely dependent on the luminosity and quality of the light in which it is viewed. That is to say that there is a direct correlation between the colour that the brain interprets and the nature of the object off which light rays are reflected and absorbed. This process is entirely mechanical. Light rays falling on the eye's retina are absorbed by the brain where they are coded and classified in terms of colour. This visible spectrum is translated graphically into the colour wheel. Traditionally the colour wheel consists of three primary colours: red, yellow and blue. When these colours are paired together in equal quantities, the binary colours of orange, green and violet are produced. Through mixing together, in varying proportions, one or more of these, all other colours are obtained. Colours on the wheel fall into two distinct areas: warm and cool.

German Expressionism ▶
Tulipa 'Orange Emperor'

On the warm, or hot, side are to be found red, orange and yellow, with the exception of lemon. Green, blue and violet, the remaining three colours, fall onto the cool side. Those colours that are positioned next to each other and that have a pigment in common are said to be in harmony. These combinations of two or more adjacent colours are pleasing to the eye, do not clash nor do they strike a harsh note. Colours appearing opposite to each other on the colour wheel also work together, but in contrast to one another. These are often referred to as complementary colours. What of course the colour wheel fails to do, which the eye readily does, is to take into account the variation in tints, shades and hues.

Unlike a painter, within whose power is the ability to reproduce colour exactly, the photographer is subject above all else to the variables of the weather with its widespread effect on colour. Colour becomes transitory. Brilliant hot sunshine will radically alter the appearance of a subject as much as intense cold. Changing light levels will effect changes of tone. Even rain is by no means a neutral agent. The soft, refreshing showers of early spring serve, particularly when linked to warm sunlight, to heighten and intensify colours. This is in direct contrast to autumnal days of solid rain when, under lowering grey skies, the world becomes almost monochromatic. As the seasons change, so too do light levels. In turn these bring about alterations in both leaf and flower colour. Evidence of this is to be found in the two images 'German Expressionism' and 'Against the Blitz'. Both possess the same tones of orange, red and green. However, in the first, the gay light colours and rich texture convey something of an air of carnival with an intensity which is both real and purposeful. In the second, as with the approach of autumn, the mood and colour are more sombre, there is warmth but it contains menace, the orange flame of the background is disturbing.

Still Life ▶
Tulipa 'General de Wet'

Notwithstanding the necessity of combating the elements, the camera, or rather the photographer, can with skill and patience, like a painter, capture a moment and thus seal a colour or colours for all time. And it is because of this that so many of the images here appear to be directly related to the world of art. We find in 'Hitchens *Flower Composition*' the exact tone of the *Papaver somniferum*. And while the setting may be different, for Hitchens belongs to the modern British movement and his painting is near abstract, the tonal qualities remain unaltered. Similarly, it is on account of the colours, violet and gold, that the *Iris reticulata* 'George' transports itself from a garden setting to become an integral part, albeit a detail, of Picasso's 1939 painting *Night Fishing at Antibes*. With 'Still Life' it is the brilliance of the tulips, daringly and dramatically placed against a trellis-seat of rich lilac-blue, itself thrown into relief by the background fence of marine-blue, that makes this such an apt subject for a painting by Broque, Cézanne or whomever.

As with the painter, and indeed the gardener, the photographer too must recognise the importance of the role of colour in any composition. It is a powerful force that, employed with intelligence, sensitivity and understanding, will act profoundly on the emotions, bringing about changes in mood and atmosphere. It is the appreciation of colour, of harmonies and contrasts, of intensity, of tone, of light influence, of the ways in which colour is distributed, combined with an awareness of texture, form and consistence, that really marks out the professional and his or her work.

After Matthew Smith (1879–1959) ▶
Tulipa 'Flair'

Lit by Flares (pages 26–7)
Tulipa 'Queen of Night'

Crumpled Tulle ▶
Rosa 'Gertrude Jekyll'

◄ Lava Lamps ▲
Lupinus 'Red Arrow', 'Prosperity', 'Lipstick Cerise' and 'Storm'

COLOUR

Picasso *Night Fishing at Antibes, 1939* (detail) ▶
Iris reticulata 'George'

Porcelain Factory (pages 32–3)
Crocus 'Remembrance'

Knicker Pink (page 36)
Dahlia 'Figurine'

Hedda Gabler, Cambridge Theatre 1970 (page 37)
Hyacinthus 'Blue Magic'

Firelock ▲
Ranunculus asiaticus

◄ Larch Wood
Melianthus major

In the Limelight ▲
Anthemis tinctoria 'E C Buxton'

Hitchens *Flower Composition* ▲
Papaver somniferum

Footlight ▲
Papaver nudicaule

Against the Blitz ▲
Crocosmia 'Lady Hamilton'

Sixties Shades ▲
Tulipa 'Fantasy'

◄ Sulphur Polypores
Tulipa 'Professor Röntgen'

Edwardian Corsage ▲
Verbascum nigrum

PATTERN

Few things in life, and life itself is no exception, are entirely random. Close inspection of our world more often than not reveals the presence of order, of uniformity and regularity, of harmony and method, of pattern. Pattern is all-embracing, universal. It has travelled through time and is evident in our art and architecture, in music and mathematics and a wide range of natural forms. Manmade or natural, pattern serves to bring rule from chaos, rigour from disparate ideas and focuses flashes of inspiration into a harmonious whole. It is the ingenious device which underpins decorative design, the foundation of classical composition and the basic structure of plant life in all its forms. Pattern enables us to make sense of what we see around us. Its very constancy provides reassurance and its strength lies in its ability to convert simple ideas into bold statements.

Ballroom Dancer ▶
Camellia x *williamsii* 'Shocking Pink'

From prehistory until the present day, pattern has been integral to all aspects of architectural and artistic detail. Dominant in the triumphant cathedrals and churches of the mediaeval ages, it survives in the grand houses of the Elizabethan era where symmetry and light are effected through a multiplicity of glass. Nearer to our own time, it is in the fanciful wealth of the Victorians, with their love of ornament, that the aggregate of pattern is to be found. Most often exuberant, rarely restrained, it becomes central to all exterior and interior decoration of the period: stone, wood and metalwork, tiling, paper and fabric, painted surfaces, even the arrangement of beds and borders in the great parks and gardens. What we see in the images here is a fusion of time, a metamorphosis, in which the character of one object is transformed into that of another. In 'Communion at Chartres' we no longer observe the detail of the dahlia, but are transported to the twelfth century where the richness of red characterises the early Gothic stained glass, and where the intention is to achieve an effect of illumination which is both secular and spiritual.

Mathematics and music provide us with the most disciplined pattern structures. Symmetry and symphony, geometry and melody, proportion and scale all have underlying principles, formulae and theories which direct and govern their various patterns. 'Love Hearts', inspired by the planting at the Château de Villandry, reshapes the traditional maze of circles into a series of fluid hearts. In their apparent motion, form is maintained and yet those box-edged borders become no less than a careless arrangement of childhood sweets, each with its potent message, which belong most properly within the pages of *Alice in Wonderland*. Similarly, the rhythmic beat of popular music, parallel avenues of trees, the linear arrangement of walls, hedges and fences that break up so much of the countryside, and the tubular bells of wind chimes all remind us of the inherent order in what first appears to be a world in confusion.

Stargazer ▶
Ipomoea 'Heavenly Blue'

Nature and pattern are complementary. The composition of the universe with its galaxies, star formations, order and purpose, is evident of this. The unerring repetition of the seasons coupled with the phases of the moon, the recurrence of the tides and the rhythm of night and day are all part of the pattern of life itself. Pattern in nature is revealed everywhere. It appears inside any single flower, often though, as in the case of 'Day-Glo', to be lost in a marked vibrancy and intensity of colour which is itself an echo of a period of thrusting, self-conscious self interest. Visible on every leaf, witness 'Green Spine Chiller', detailed in feather and fur, scale and skin, it reverberates in birdsong, in the movement of water, and is as much a part of the frosty spider's web as it is of the night sky.

Captured in the images that follow is a highly individualistic look at patterning in many different forms. Here we are invited to observe rarely seen, intimate close-ups of petal formations, demonstrated in 'Ballroom Dancer' where the aptly-named Camellia x *williamsii* 'Shocking Pink' takes to the dance floor to engage us in the delights of Latin America and Charleston. In contrast, 'Puckered Pink Satin' declares the party over. Passion spent, discarded skirts lie incongruous on a silent floor. Detail of leaf structure, outlined in 'Gorgeous Green Taffeta', gives us entry into the world of theatre, of costume and foreign courts, while that of bark, beautifully betrayed in 'Ghostly Convoy', carries with it a message thrilling yet sinister. In silent, frozen waters, unknown ships glide with stealth and menace, watching and unwatched. These, together with the exciting, at times disturbing, sculptures of 'Ice-capped Maidens', redolent of a near-forgotten age, and 'One Step Ahead of the Rest', where severed heads await redemption, all reveal not only the artist at work, but unexpected and beguiling pattern magic.

Inca Empire ▶
Helianthus annuus 'Titan'

Communion at Chartres ▲
Dahlia 'Long's Red Admiral'

Partial Eclipse ▲
Helianthus annuus 'Titan'

Magdalen Moon ▲
Magdalen Bridge from Oxford Botanic Garden

The Thin Blue Line ▲
Cabbages and chard, Château de Villandry, France

◄ Catherine Wheel on Watered Silk
Helleborus orientalis

Love Hearts ▲
The Garden of Love, Château de Villandry, France

◄ Green Spine Chiller
Matteuccia struthiopteris

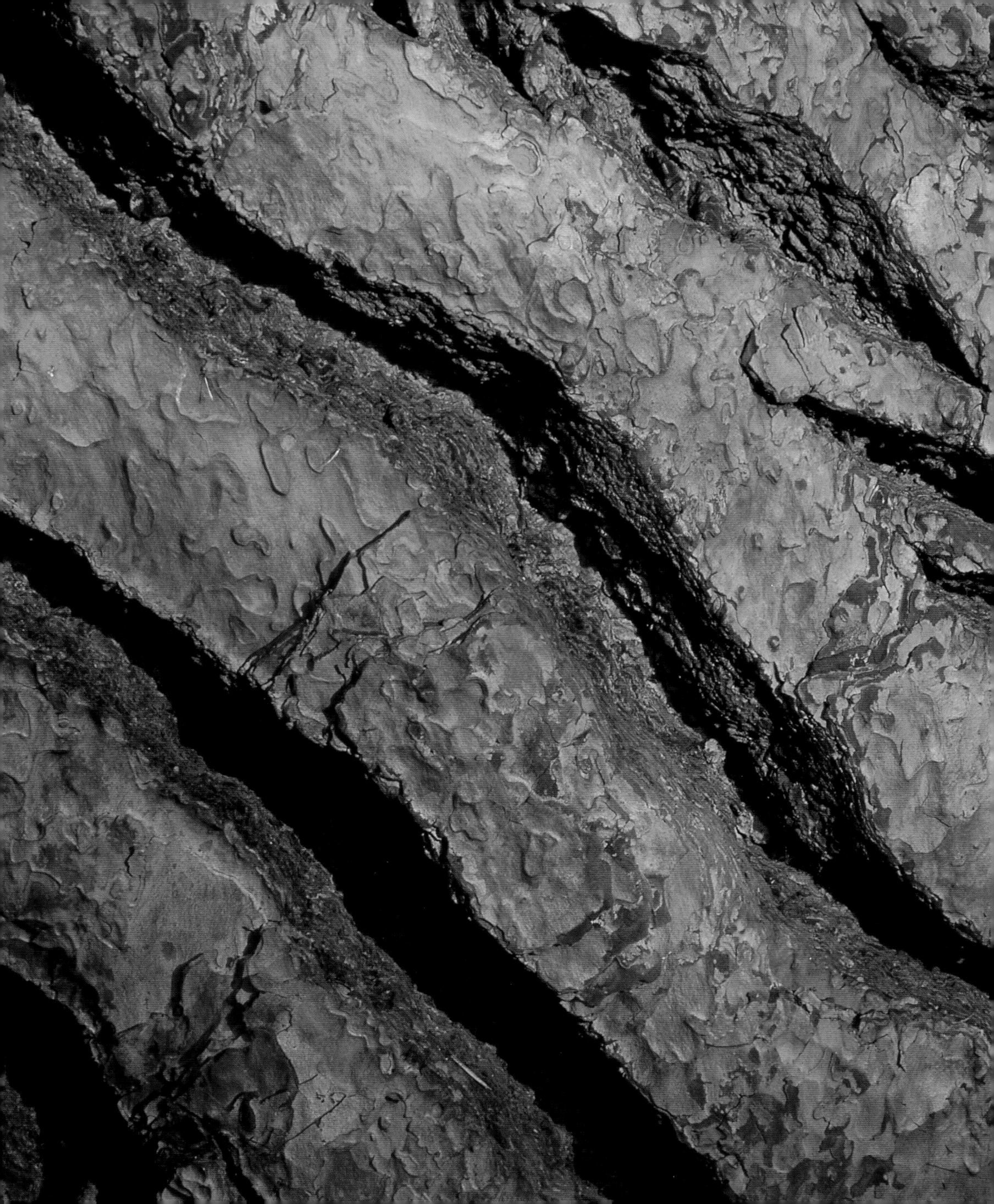

Two Directional ▲
Prunus serrula

◄ Ploughed Pine
Pinus pinea

Day-Glo ▲

Gazania 'Sunset Jane'

Wood Shavings ▲
Ranunculus asiaticus

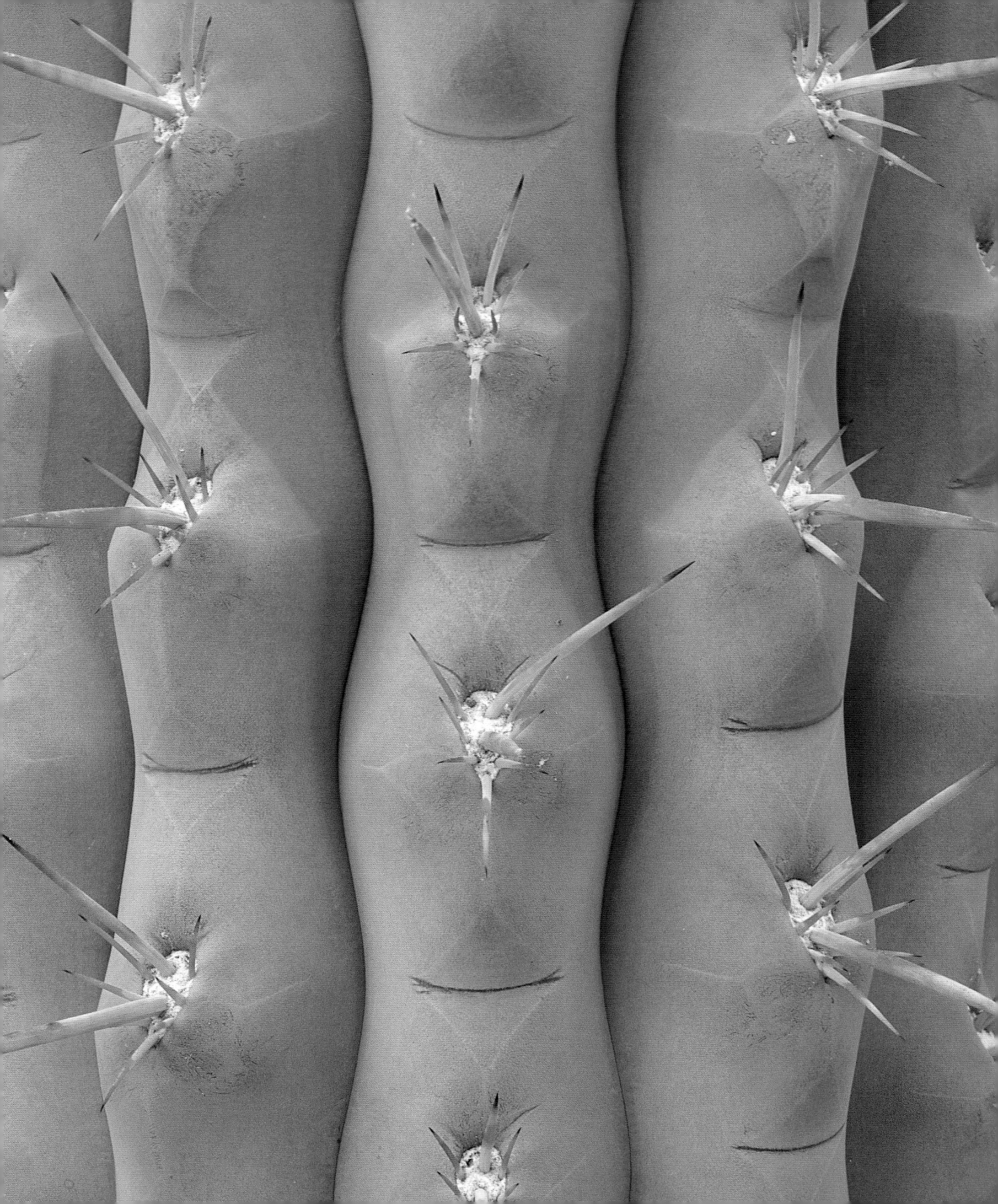

◀ Body Piercing
Browningia hartlingianus

Desert Highway ▲
Pachycereus pringlei

A Fanfare of Pipes ▲
Chrysanthemum 'Louisa'

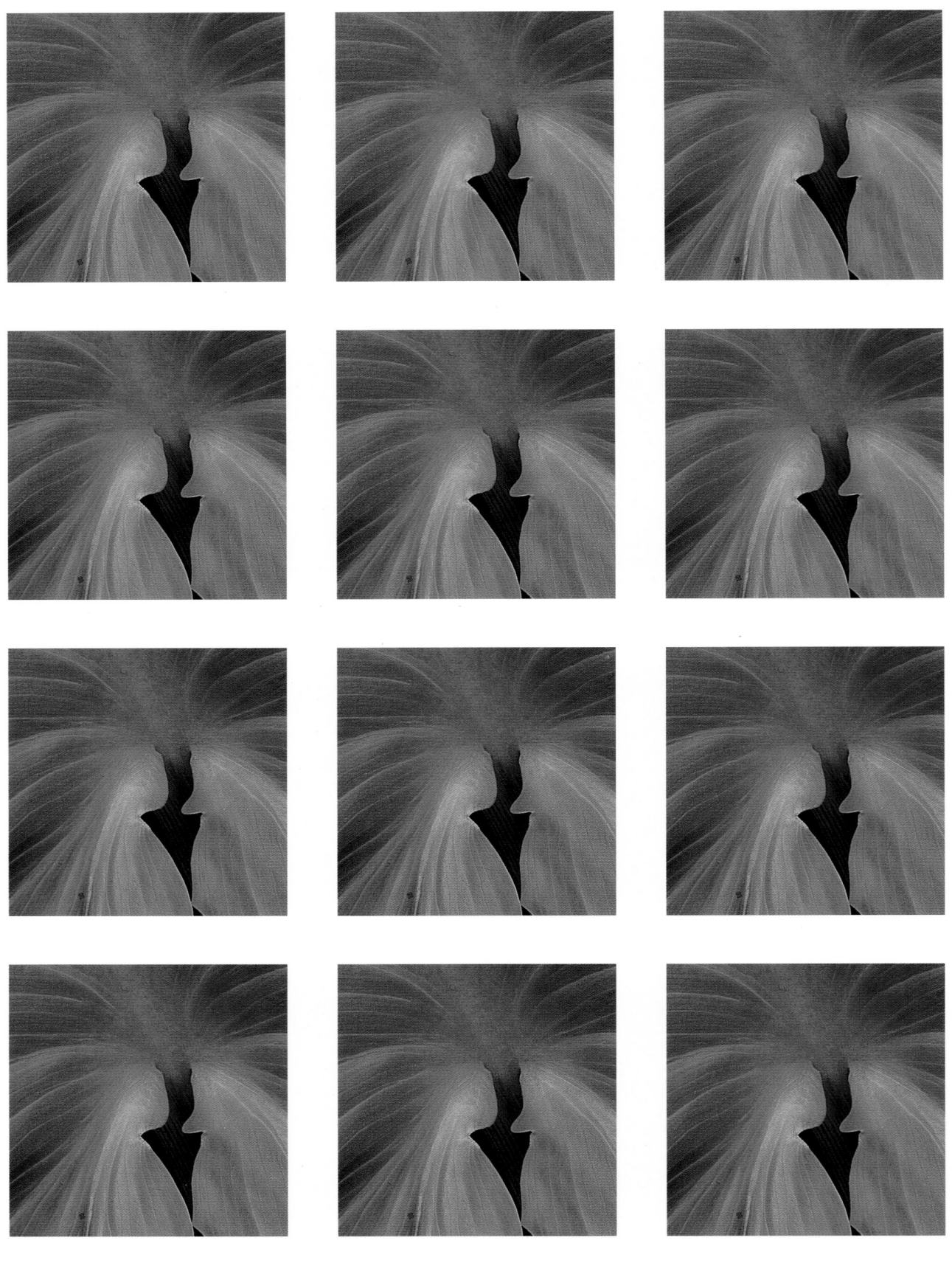

▲ Gorgeous Green Taffeta ▶

Zantedeschia aethiopica

Puckered Pink Satin ▶
Rosa 'Gertrude Jekyll'

Body Armour (pages 72–3)
Agave parryii, Huntington Botanical Gardens, Los Angeles

Super Nova (pages 74–5)
Echium wildpretii

Ice-capped Maidens ▲
Statues for sale at Sprivers Garden, Kent

Ghostly Convoy (pages 76–7)
Betula utilis

One Step Ahead of the Rest ▲
Deities by Patricia Volk

FORM

The very essence of an object is inherent in its form. Its existence is dependent upon its shape. Without this structural unity, design or arrangement, the mind struggles to understand what it sees, fails to fashion connections. But there is nothing arbitrary about form, nothing capricious, the result of an accident. It is the development of principle, the evolution of basic shapes, of straight and curved lines which, at their simplest, are represented as squares and circles. Within the two-dimensional these may be further refined to give us, in mathematical terms, rectangles, triangles, parallelograms, hexagons and octagons. In three-dimensional form, we are able to construct cubes, cylinders, pyramids and spheres. However, whatever the degree of complexity of shape of the objects with which we surround ourselves, there exist constant and recurring themes and it is these that we look for, recognise and which make familiar what would otherwise be obscure and unintelligible.

In Mourning ▶
Aquilegia vulgaris

Such themes frequent the natural world, are present in our universe. We observe them in the shape of the planets, of the sun, the moon and the stars, of comets which trail across the sky at night. They are to be found in the depths of the ocean, in the shells made up of concentric circles, the starfish beached at low tide, the eggs of spawning fish. Present in the shape of the trees of woodland and forest, they are detailed too in their leaves, best described as oblong, orbicular, ovate, even rhomboidal. In the simple daisy, we recognise both circle and ellipse; the human body recalls the rectangle.

It comes as little surprise to find that these fundamental forms are regularly repeated in nature, often appearing in totally changed circumstances. So, in the image of ruby chard, the blood-red, linear stems of the edible vegetable are, in effect, of the same construction as the aorta, that great artery issuing from the left ventricle of the heart. Similarly, the component form of *Kniphofia triangularis* is represented in 'Prize Bunch' as a hand of bananas, albeit strangely coloured, or award-winning carrots on display at the village show. A further example of this link is demonstrated in 'Embryo', 'Birth', 'Infancy' and 'Coming of Age' where the sequence of the opening of the bulbous *Nectaroscordum siculum* parallels in part the early stages of man.

Manmade structures invariably are based on some unifying order. From the cooling towers employed in the production of nuclear-powered energy to the baby's rattle discovered among the ashes of pompeii, the underlying shapes remain both recognisable and known. Witness the design of Evans and Shalev for the Tate Gallery, St. Ives, Cornwall, where two basic forms, the cylinder and rectangle, the first recalling the former gasometer, the second an earlier development, have resulted in a building at the forefront of the modernist movement.

Ladies Day at Ascot ▶
Magnolia campbellii 'Charles Raffill'

In much the same way, the glass pyramidal structure in front of The Louvre in Paris is inextricably linked to the pyramids of ancient Egypt. In Mondrian's *Composition, 1929* we see an experiment in equilibrium where primary colours are separated from one another with straight horizontal and vertical lines.

Such constructions of man are not without natural partners, an idea explored in many of the images here. In focusing on the detail to be found at the centre of the oriental poppy, *Papaver orientale* 'Patty's Plum', we are, in effect, looking directly into the engine of a turbo jet. Millinery joins hands with nature in 'Ladies Day at Ascot' when the outline shape of the flowering *Magnolia campbellii* 'Charles Raffill' adopts the texture, style and elegance of a model hat worn at the races. What is apparent is that universal shapes, many of which are to be found readily in the natural world, become the basic building blocks for all that is manmade. Therefore, *Tropaeolum tricolorum*, a member of the nasturtium family, becomes gaily coloured windsocks, frosted *Euphorbia characias* subsp. *wulfenii* are abandoned mopheads left out in the cold, while the brilliant stems of *Cornus sanguinea* 'Winter Flame' are transformed into the plastic pieces belonging to a child's construction kit.

All of the images here delight in intimacy. We are encouraged to inspect closely, to delve deeply into an unlocked box of highly original, thoughtfully presented pictures where each subject, whether it is known to us or not, reveals from within itself understandable and recognisable form.

Turbo Jet ▶
Papaver orientale 'Patty's Plum'

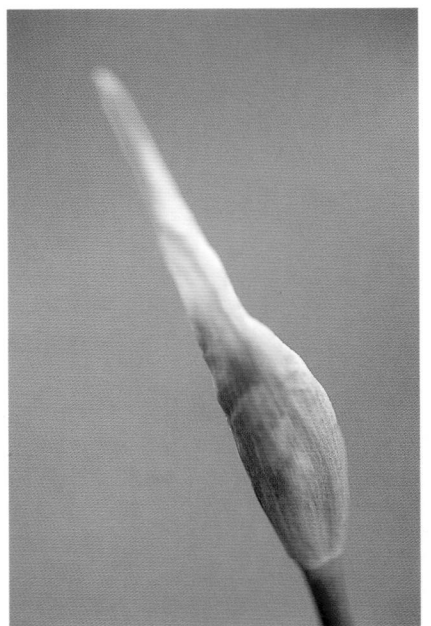  

Embryo, Birth, Infancy, Coming of Age ▲ ▶
Nectaroscordum siculum

Punk ▲

Clematis orientalis

Wax Tapers ▲

Garrya elliptica

Iced Mopheads ▲
Euphorbia characias subsp. *wulfenii*

Crystallised Daisies ▲
Euphorbia x *martinii*

Filigree ▲
Plane trees, Lake Como, Italy

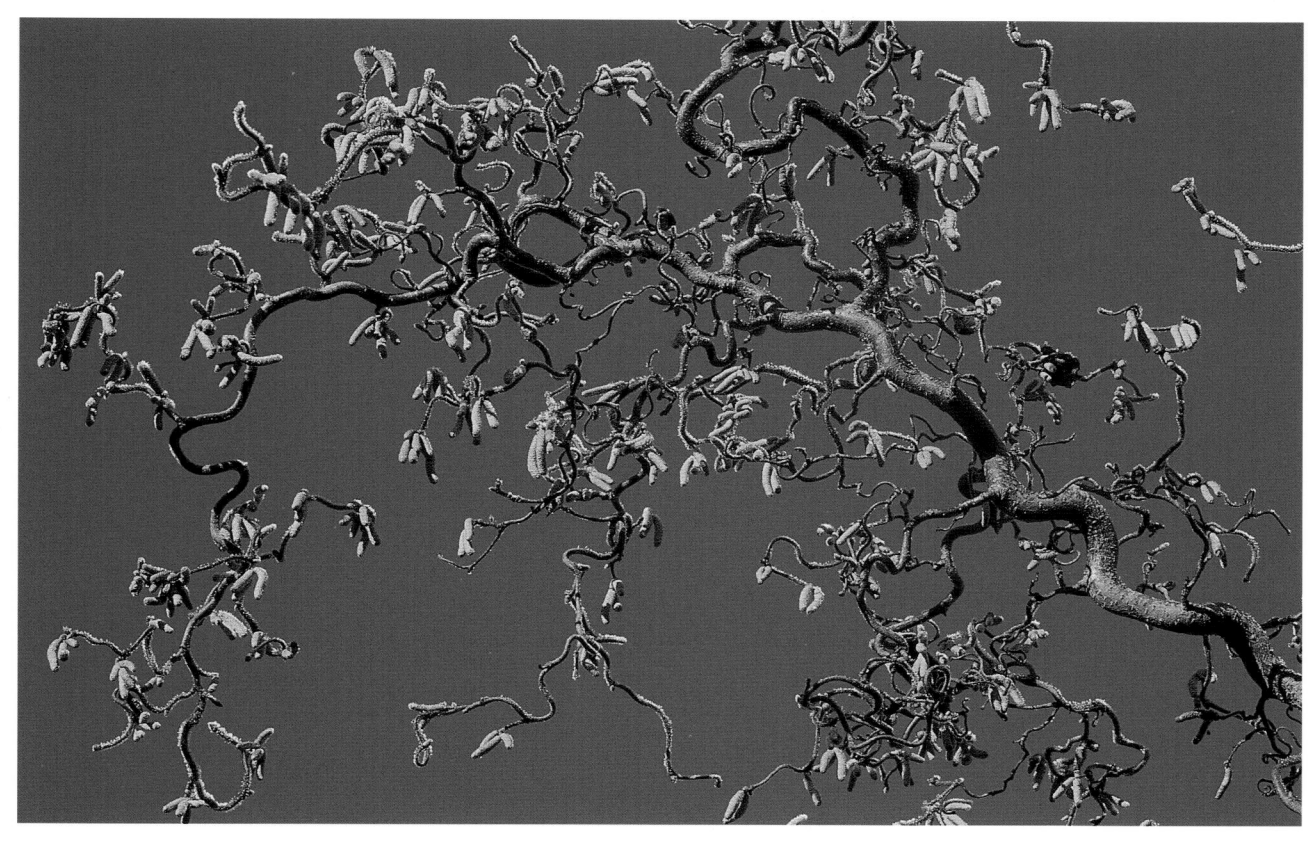

Costume Jewellery ▲

Corylus avellana 'Contorta'

Eastern Sweetmeats ▲
Lupinus 'Paddington Bear'

Prize Bunch ▲
Kniphofia triangularis

Sealing Wax ▲
Rosa moyesii 'Geranium'

Butterfly Nut Attired ▶
Parrotia persica

Tomato on the Vine ▲

Papaver orientale

Inflight Fuelling ▲
Salvia fulgens

◄ Windsocks
Tropaeolum tricolorum

Construction Kit ▲
Cornus sanguinea 'Winter Flame'

Aorta ▲
Ruby chard

Blood Molecules ▲
Hippeastrum

◄ Helter Skelter
Canna 'Striata'

Sherbert Dip (page 106)
Hemerocallis 'Perennial Pleasure'

Furled Parasol (page 107)
Muscari armeniacum

Classical Urn at Sunset ▲
Tulipa 'Ballerina'

◀ Ripe Fruit
Iris foetidissima

LIGHT

Light is the agency by which and through which objects are made visible. Its nature is iridescent, that is to say it divides out into colour, colour which is translated into the rainbow with its familiar hues of red, orange, yellow, green, blue, indigo and violet. Different colours possess different frequencies, with long waves, such as red, bending far less than short waves like violet. In photographic terms, as in painting, it is the tone, the relative lightness or darkness of a subject, that becomes the essential tool through which the relative effects of light may be expressed. Empty husks of *Stipa gigantea,* 'Flickering Flame', shot against the light are thrown into partial silhouette so that, with a reduction in the amount of visible colour, the tonal pattern of the subject is emphasised. The resulting metaphor is readily understood. The seed-carrying stems of the grass are easily imagined as firelight in possession of warmth, energy and not least illumination.

Surrealism ▶
Frosted ruby chard

For the photographer at work outdoors, and one of the strengths of all these images is that they are shot in situ and not, as may be believed, in the studio, the quality of light will depend not simply on the time of day but also on season and weather. Natural light, emitted by the sun, is subject to variation, a variation often as dramatic as it is sudden.

Spring light has a gentle quality. It is soft, alluring, soothing to the eye, mild in disposition. And in the garden, after the bleakness of the winter months, spring-flowering plants with blues and yellows in abundance make bold and welcome statements. Morning dew, or the unexpected shower of warm rain, simply serve to highlight the mystical character of the garden at this time of year. This is the season of impressions, caught here in 'Spring Galaxy', where countless jewel-like crocuses contribute a startling luminosity to a stretch of lawn. Similarly 'Impressionism', wonderful wide drifts of red and yellow tulips, immediately recalls the work of painters like Monet, Seurat and Signac.

With the lengthening of days and the growing intensity of the sun, summer light levels become denser, more concentrated, at times unremittingly harsh. Early mornings and evenings provide respite from the glare and afford opportunities to achieve remarkable effects. We observe this in images such as 'Uplighter' where a single flower of *Anthemis tinctoria* 'E C Buxton' is suffused in a warm glow of light, or in 'Pink Plastic' where the tonal quality of the petals of *Echinacea purpurea* 'Rubinstern' disregard the natural world and become manmade. *'How Green Was My Valley'* has a profundity which owes all to the action of the camera one daybreak in a small, forgotten corner of Wales.

Molten Ore ▶
Red oak leaf

Autumn sees a drawing in, a closing down, the onset of shadows, of mists, of cold, first frosts, in short a subtle but consistent change. But it is not without its glory. Strong sunlight may be no more, but in its place is an often shadowless diffused light which opens up a wealth of opportunity. Detail is maximised and the richness of the late season leaf, berry and bark impact all around. Leaf colour is particularly strong as is evident in both 'Chinese Lacquer' and 'Molten Ore'. The first, the leaves of *Acer cappadocicum* 'Rubrum', appear sumptuously varnished; the second, a leaf of the red oak, is mineral made liquid by fire. In different mood, the frosted bloom of the 'Rosemary Rose' carries its message 'Last of Summer' unequivocally.

Winter brings its own lighting effects. Sharp frosts and heavy falls of snow, the air cold and still, pure skies and strong light all excite interest. The world is more clearly defined, free from obstruction, claims greater transparency. None of this is lost to the camera. '*A Winter's Tale*' speaks for itself. In the grounds of the Palladian Chiswick House, Lord Burlington's snow-covered statues and urns are thrown into sharp relief against the dramatically dark yew hedges that surround them. The flat winter light creates a near monochromatic image washed imperceptibly with blue. That same wood-smoke blue chills 'Cold Charmian', Cleopatra's handmaid, far removed from Egypt's warm embrace.

Evident throughout the images here is the way in which light has been manipulated. The pictures show an awareness of tonal quality, an appreciation of light and shade, a deep understanding of not only the subtlety of light but also of its power and force. These qualities elevate the pictures into the realms of art.

Chinese Lacquer ▶
Acer cappadocicum 'Rubrum'

Impressionism (pages 116–7)
Tulips, Gardens of Mainau, Lake Constance

Uplighter ▲
Anthemis tinctoria 'E C Buxton'

◄ *How Green Was My Valley*
Dolwen, Powys, Wales

Cold Charmian ▲

Sculpture by Helen Sinclair, The Arrow Cottage Garden, Herefordshire

Dresden Detail ▲

Tulipa 'Angélique'

Sparkling Wine ▲
Camellia sasanqua 'Sparkling Burgundy'

Pink Plastic ▲
Echinacea purpurea 'Rubinstern'

A Winter's Tale ▲
Chiswick House, London

Chilled History ▲
Hatfield House, Hertfordshire

◄ Silent Witness
Statue of Venus, Rousham Landscape Garden, Oxfordshire

Fairy Lanterns ▲
Leucojum aestivum 'Gravetye Giant'

Art Nouveau ▲
Galanthus 'Atkinsii'

Blown Glass ▲
Allium sphaerocephalon

◄ Spring Galaxy
Crocus tomasinianus

Quietism ▲
Tulipa 'Don Quichotte'

Last of Summer ▲
Rosa 'Rosemary Rose'

Flickering Flame ▲
Stipa gigantea

◄ At Home with Miss Havisham
Cobweb, Ridley's Cheer, Wiltshire

Dipped in Sugar ▶
Astrantia major 'Hadspen Blood'

TEXTURE

Texture determines our response to the multitude of surfaces and substances that occur and that we encounter in our daily lives. It is the structural impression that results from the manner of combining or interrelating the parts of a whole. Without it, objects become devoid of interest, assume an insignificance, are unworthy of note. Texture is the disposition of components of a body. It translates in everyday language in words like rough, gnarled, furrowed, smooth, silken, velvety. Often these appear as a series of contrasts, of opposites, so hard becomes linked with soft, wet coupled to dry, sharp to blunt. But it is in association with the five senses that texture carries its greatest impact, and none more so than with touch.

Punctured Plastic ▶
Prunus serrula

Through touch we learn to appreciate the quality of what is around us. Touch becomes a point of reference, a signal to be understood and interpreted. So, the flower of the globe artichoke comes to symbolise 'Pompon', a fluffy, woolly ball. We are children returned to the classroom. Armed with scissors, cardboard disk and a skein of unwanted wool, we wind and cut, the warmth of the fibre reassuringly caressing our skin. With 'Bolt of Silk', we reject the stem of the ruby chard and are transported to the Aladdin's cave of the draper's shop. Here we run eager fingers through a plethora of silks and satins, cashmeres and mohairs, muslin and calico, the touch of each creating new and unexpected sensations.

No less important are the associations to be made with texture of the remaining senses. Seeing is in itself immediately suggestive. In observing the 'Soapy Spines' of *Aloe polyphylla*, we recognise the leaf ends as sharp to the touch. To extract the fragrant essences will, we know, cause pain. Fallen leaves resonate under foot in the autumnal wood, a detail recalled in 'Scorched Earth'. In a wider context we experience a barren landscape, traces of snow lingering on freshly ploughed land. That the palette requires to be stimulated by texture as well as by taste is not lost on our best chefs. The most exciting and appetising of dishes continue to take this into account. In 'Savoy at Midnight' the hoar frost has taken its toll on the cabbage leaf. Already we discern the rottenness, the onset of decay filters into our nostrils – we recoil.

Within the garden, the source of all of the images here, the role of texture remains of paramount importance. The ambitious gardener demands more of his or her plants than solely colour or simply form. Texture adds drama and magnetism to borders. The positioning of plants becomes an integral part of a plan where leaf shape may count for more than flower.

Paper Lanterns ▶
Fritillaria imperialis 'Orange Perfection'

Evidence of this is apparent in the very different leaves depicted in 'Pleated Velours', 'Exotic Plumage' and 'Elephant Hide'. Similarly, the designed garden takes into account a relationship between hard and soft landscaping, between the cutting edge of a flagged path and the billowing catmint that lines it. On a broader canvas, a marked contrast in texture is to be found between the summer and winter gardens. The former is awash with ephemera, the latter uncompromisingly stark. To this end, witness the different barks shown in 'Shale Stratum' and 'Charcoal and Sepia Wash'.

Such is the intensity of the images that follow, it requires little effort to consider them in the light of the remaining senses. Indeed the power of each individual picture demands an explanation that goes way beyond the casual glance. In 'Country House Curtains', for example, while we may have little inclination to taste the fabric, we can readily conjure up the smells associated with a material that has hung at the same closed windows for countless generations. Here is a mustiness that combines the perceptive reek of damp with the odour of moth balls, an absence of airiness, of newness. And at the approach of darkness, at the drawing down of blinds, at the rattle of tarnished rings on wooden pole, at the rustle of damask and the swish of silk, we know with a certainty the people, the place and the hour. For this is the power of the camera, the inspiration of the subject and the artistry of the eye behind the lens.

Mellow Fruitfulness ▶
Pumpkin

Scorched Earth ▲
Rodgersia pinnata 'Elegans'

Fibre Optics ▶
Hordeum jubatum

Shale Stratum ▲
Pinus nigra subsp. *maritima*

◄ Charcoal and Sepia Wash
Betula utilis

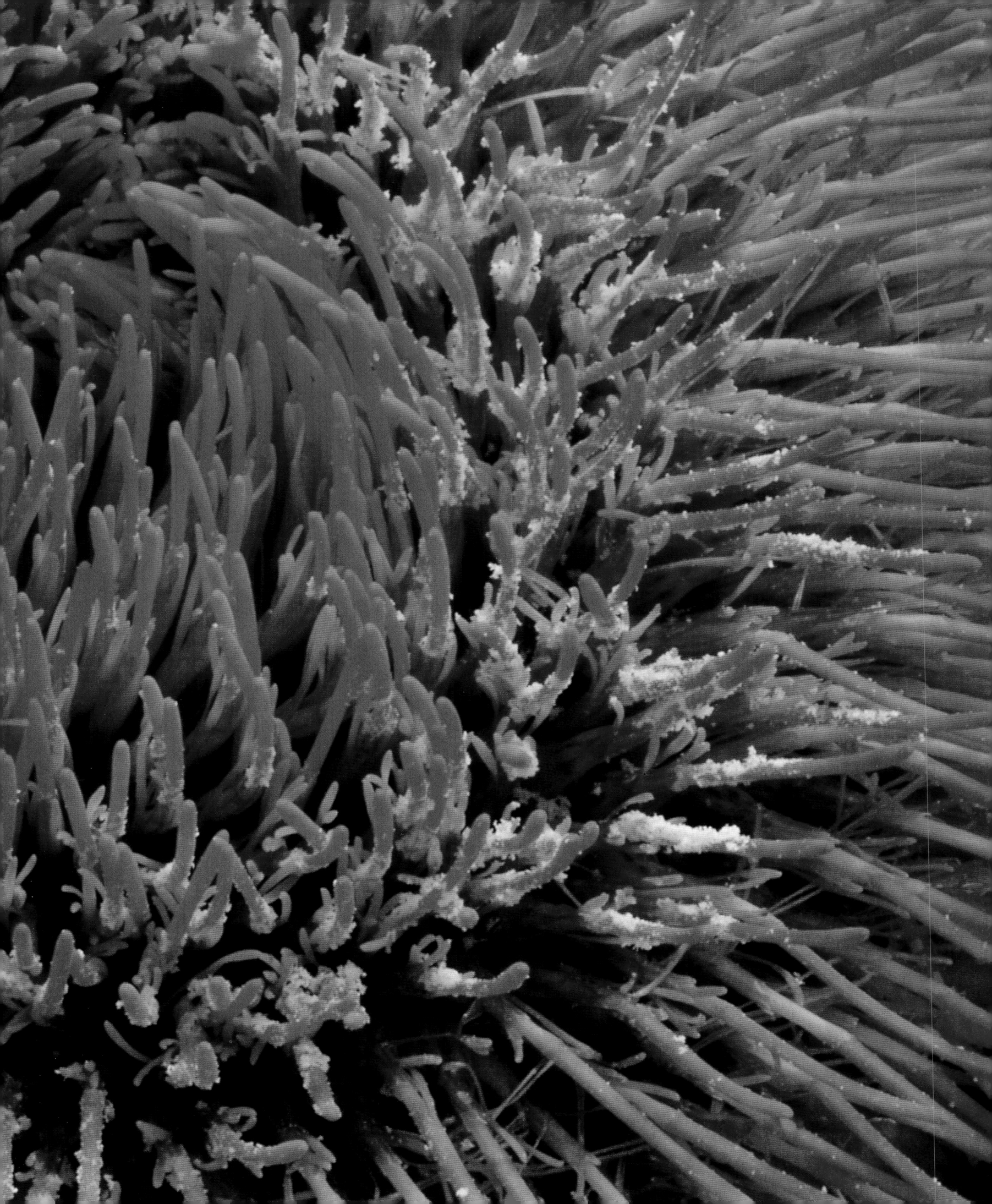

Pompon (pages 148–9)
Flower of globe artichoke

Sabres Rattling ▶
Ophiopogon planiscapus 'Nigrescens'

Savoy at Midnight (pages 152–3)
Frosted cabbage

Exotic Plumage (pages 154–5)
Canna 'Striata'

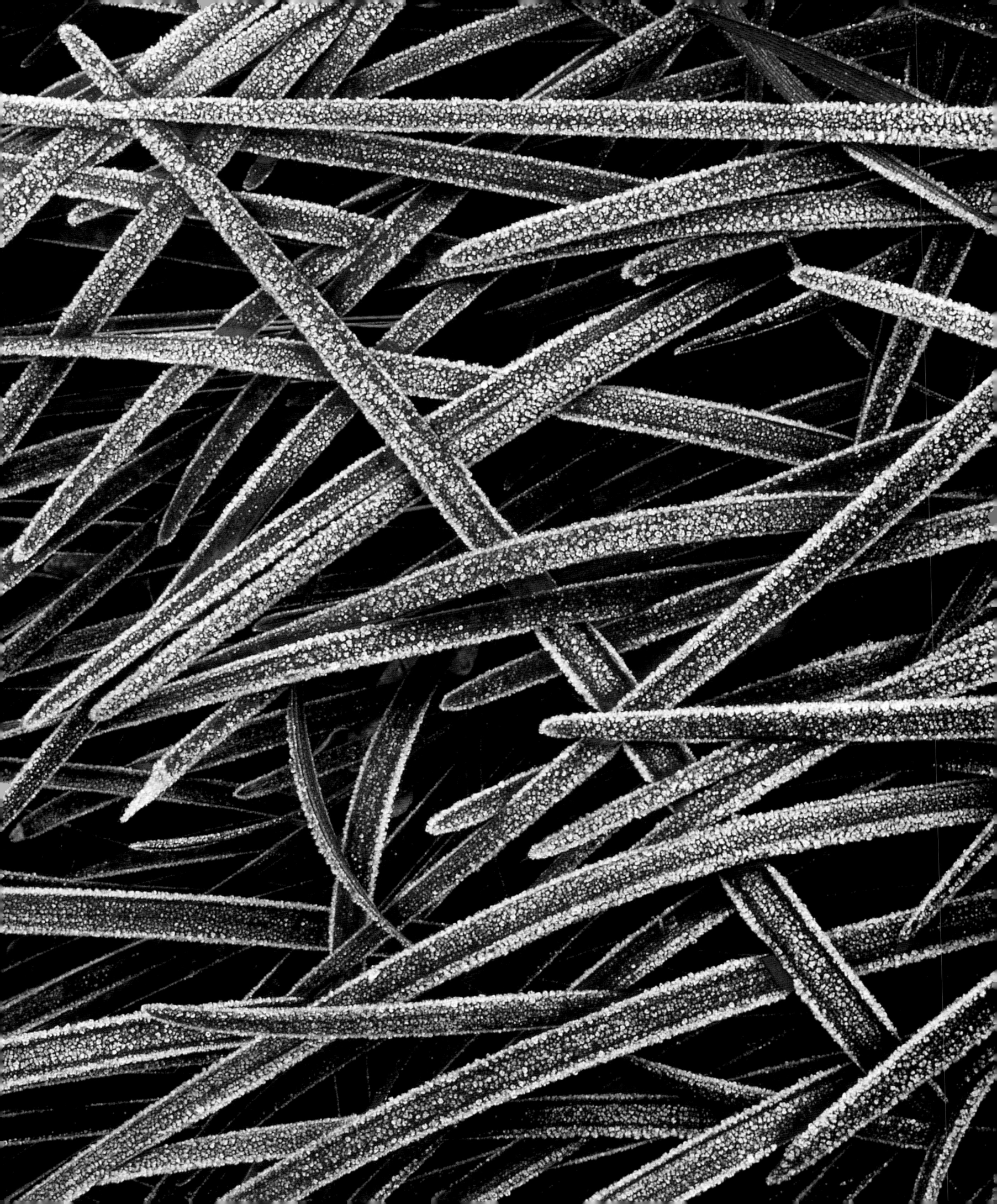

Pleated Velours ▲
Philodendron melanochrysum

Soapy Spines (pages 156–7)
Aloe polyphylla

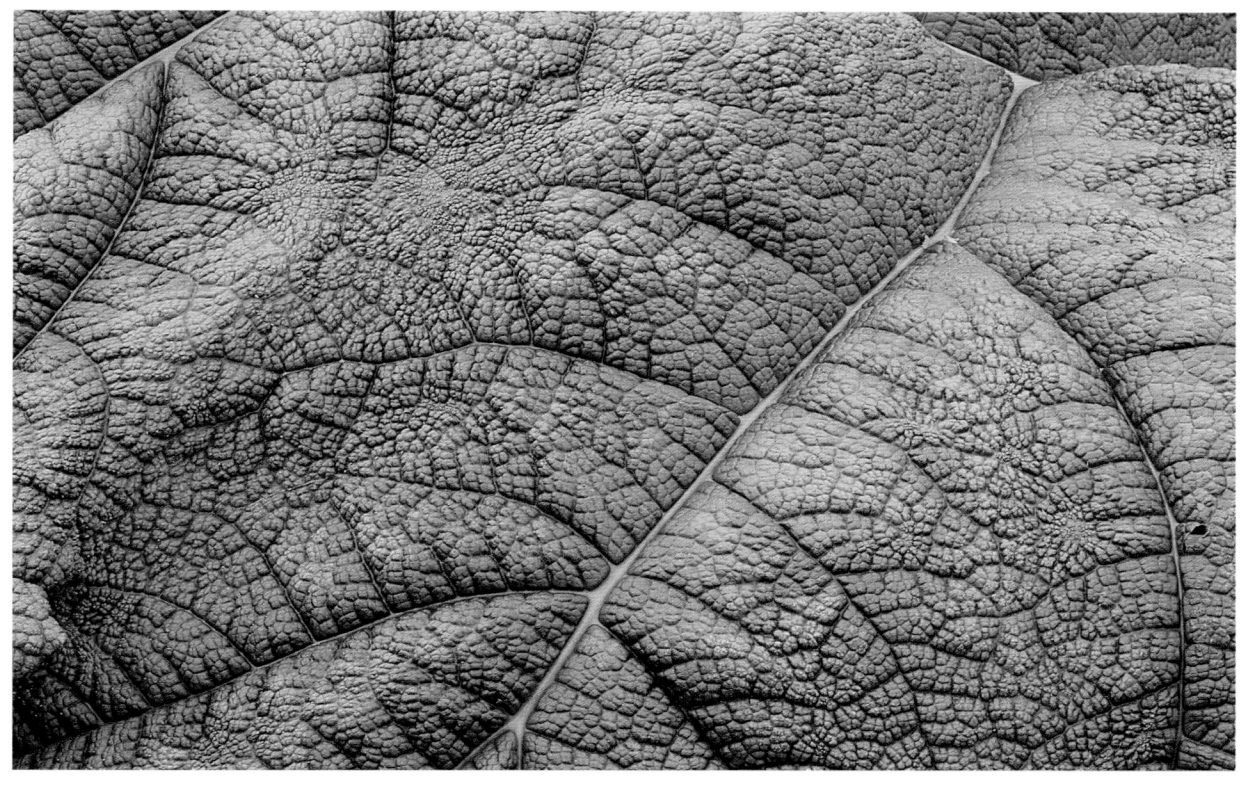

Elephant Hide ▲

Gunnera manicata

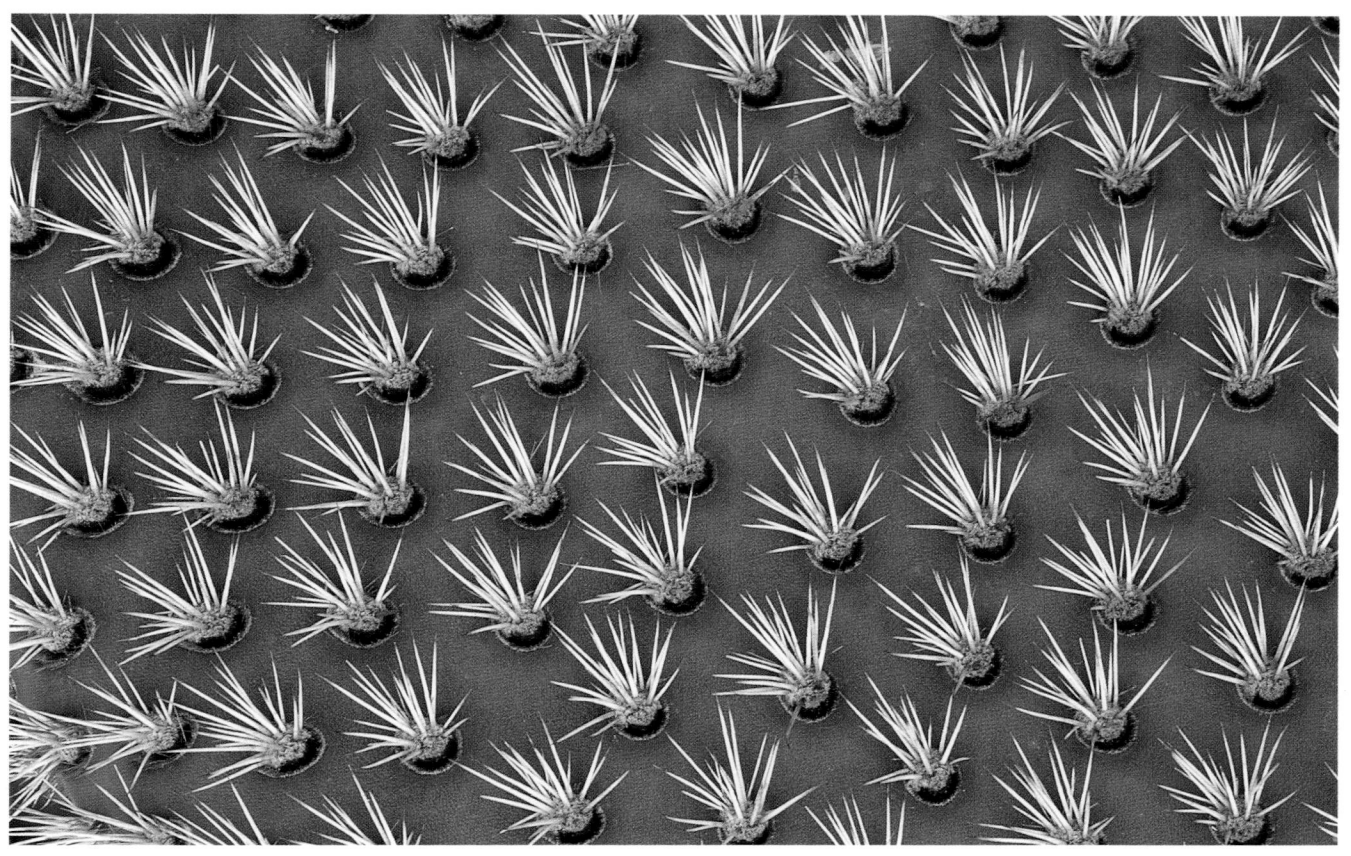

Pincushion ▲
Opuntia pycnantha

◄ Country House Curtains
Acer capillipes

Liberty Print (pages 162–3)
Cephalocereus senilis

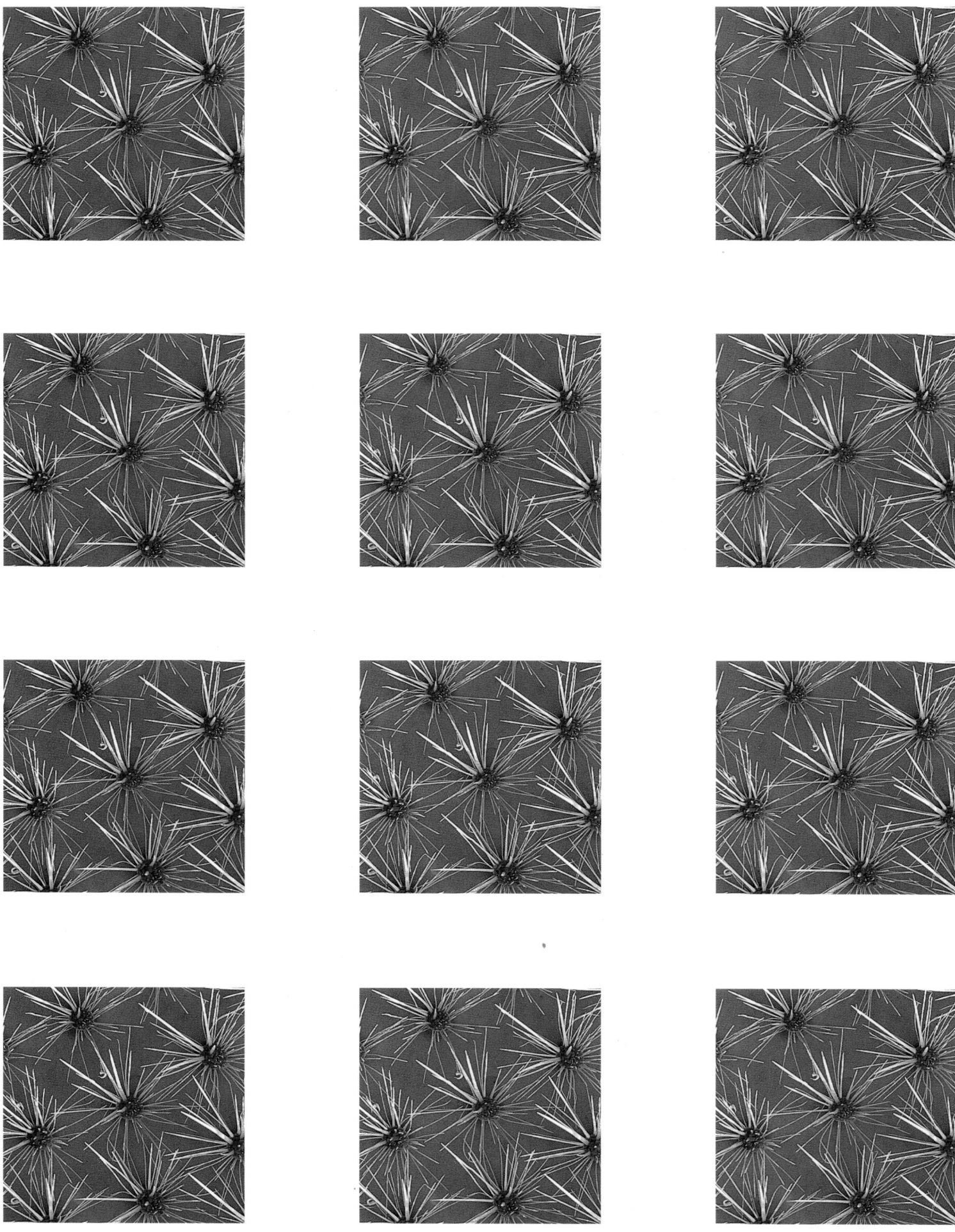

Skin Disease ▲
Ruby chard

Arterial Bruising ▲
Rheum palmatum

Cartier Brooch ▶
Ornamental cabbage

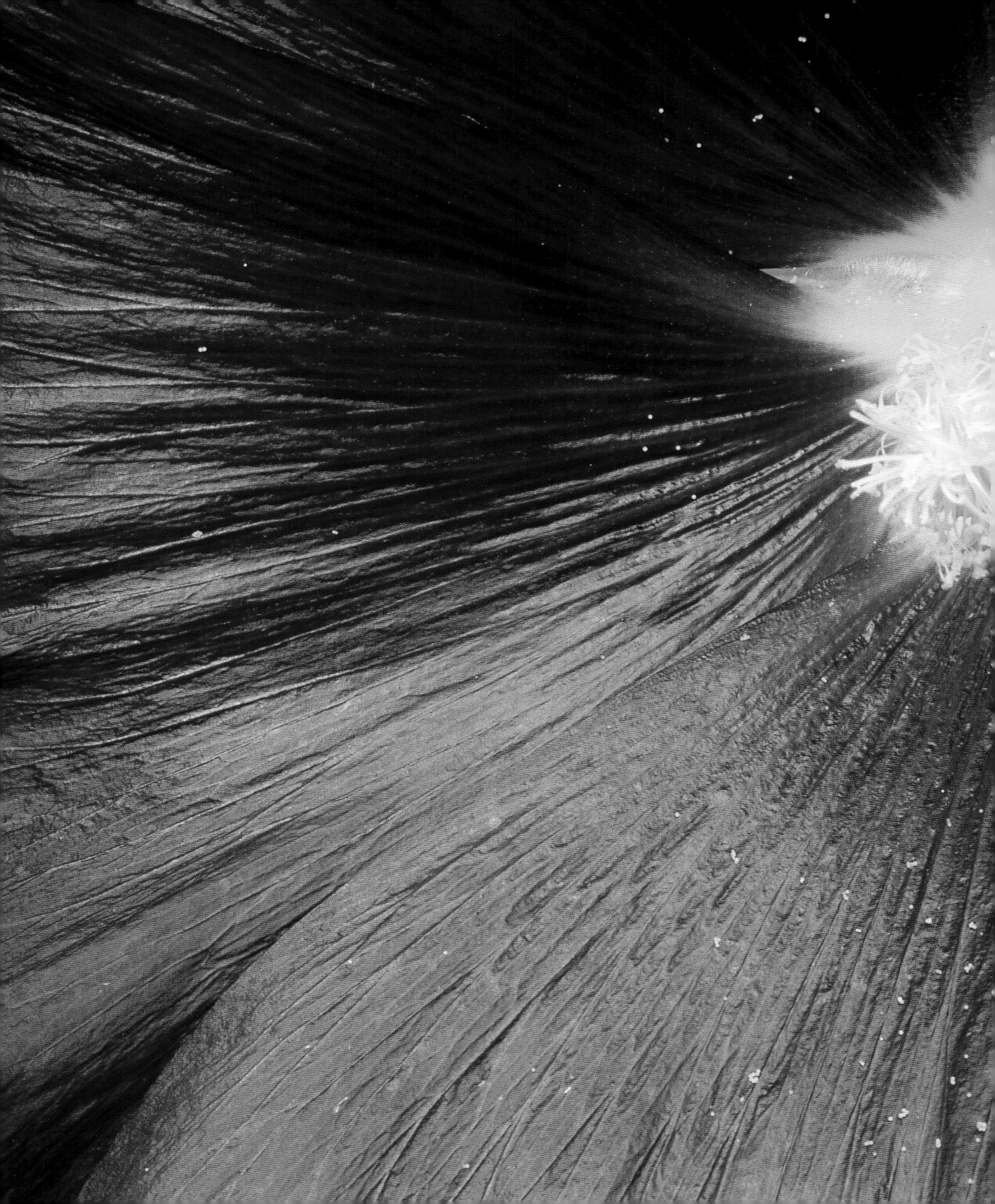

◄ Spotlight on Satin
Alcea rosea 'Nigra'

Bolt of Silk ▶
Ruby chard

BUTTER CHURN (page 1)
Yellow ranunculus
The attraction of the ranunculus is the purity of colour and the way in which each flower unfurls from the centre. Each one is different from another, which makes them especially fascinating.
Olympus OM2, 90mm macro lens with 31mm extension tube, f22, Fujichrome Velvia film

SWEET VALENTINE (pages 2–3)
Centre of red rose
A near-perfect red rose, the delight of which is the wonderfully saturated colour of the bloom, coupled with its precise symmetry.
Olympus OM2, 90mm macro lens with 31mm extension tube, f22, Fujichrome Velvia film

MOODY BLUES (pages 4–5)
Blue hyacinth
The scent of these alluring hyacinths is almost detectable. Suitable for indoor cultivation, or outside, hyacinths are available in a wide range of lovely colours. Shot at f4, the background is thrown out of focus to concentrate attention on the flower heads in the foreground.
Olympus OM2, 90mm macro lens with 31mm extension tube, f4, Fujichrome Velvia film

FINALE (pages 6–7)
Orange dahlia
In order to show the entire dahlia in sharp focus, it was necessary to set the smallest aperture possible (f22) on the macro lens to maximise the depth of field. Although this gave a slow shutter speed of half a second, an absence of wind prevented any subject movement.
Olympus OM2, 90mm macro lens, f22, Fujichrome Velvia film

COXCOMB (pages 10–11)
Dahlia **'David Howard'**
Photographing extreme close-ups is highly specialised. Because of the high magnification required, a tripod and cable release are necessary to avoid camera shake. Depth of field is reduced and focusing becomes extremely critical. In order to arrest movement caused by a strong wind, in this instance a shutter speed of 1/500 second was selected, the picture taken at f4.
Olympus OM2, 90mm macro lens with 31mm extension tube, f4, Fujichrome Velvia film

GERMAN EXPRESSIONISM (page 21)
Tulipa **'Orange Emperor'**
Growing in a border at the Keukenhof Gardens in Holland, this tulip is shot against a sea of spring forget-me-nots, the blue serving to complement the orange. The tulip is isolated with a macro lens and, by employing a large aperture (f4), the background is thrown out of focus.
Olympus OM2, 90mm macro lens, f4, Fujichrome Velvia film

STILL LIFE (page 23)
Tulipa **'General de Wet'**
An all-time favourite, the brilliant orange of 'General de Wet' works well in a container. Here it is set against the blue of a trellis seat, a number of the flower heads bent forward with the weight of rain.
Pentax 67, 105mm lens, f22, Fujichrome Velvia film

AFTER MATTHEW SMITH (1879–1959) (page 25)
Tulipa **'Flair'**
To isolate the heads of these tulips in the Keukenhof Gardens in Holland, a 75–210 zoom with an aperture of f8 was used. This involved crouching with the tripod so that the actual shooting took place through flowers placed in the foreground.
Olympus OM2, 75–210mm zoom lens, f8, Fujichrome Velvia film

LIT BY FLARES (pages 26–7)
Tulipa **'Queen of Night'**
In this spring border, silver artemisia contrasts sharply with the deep plum of the tulip, 'Queen of Night', and the brilliant orange of tulip 'Ballerina'. Shooting at a low level allowed for a couple of the 'Ballerina' tulips to be either side of the viewfinder. An aperture of f8 threw them beautifully out of focus.
Olympus OM2, 75–210mm zoom lens, f8, Fujichrome Velvia film.

CRUMPLED TULLE (page 29)
Rosa **'Gertrude Jekyll'**
A lovely and reliable rose introduced by David Austin in 1986 and named after the famous gardener, Gertrude Jekyll (1843–1932). Its beauty lies not only in its shape but also its fragrance. This specimen was taken in a light drizzle.
Olympus OM2, 90mm macro lens, f22, Fujichrome Velvia film

LAVA LAMPS (pages 30–1)
Lupinus **'Red Arrow'**
Traditionally associated with the cottage garden, lupins provide a welcome splash of colour in early summer before the main herbaceous border plants come into their own. These, of exotic colour, were growing at the Devonshire nursery of Sarah Conibear whose company, Westcountry Lupins, is the only outlet supplying individually coloured lupin plantlets by mail order.
Olympus OM2, 90mm macro lens, f4, Fujichrome Velvia film

LAVA LAMPS (pages 30–1)
Lupinus **'Prosperity'**
See description above.
Olympus OM2, 90mm macro lens, f4, Fujichrome Velvia film

LAVA LAMPS (pages 30–1)
Lupinus 'Lipstick Cerise'
See description above.
Olympus OM2, 90mm macro lens, f4, Fujichrome Velvia film

LAVA LAMPS (pages 30–1)
Lupinus 'Storm'
See description above.
Olympus OM2, 90mm macro lens, f4, Fujichrome Velvia film

PORCELAIN FACTORY (pages 32–3)
Crocus 'Remembrance'
To open fully, the spring crocuses require a warm, sunny day. The soft light, brought about by waiting for cloud to diffuse the sun, highlights the rich colour of the petals and central structures.
Olympus OM2, 90mm macro lens, f22, Fujichrome Velvia film

PICASSO *NIGHT FISHING AT ANTIBES, 1939* (detail) (page 35)
Iris reticulata 'George'
The abstract quality of this image was achieved with the use of a 200mm macro lens, focusing on the front of the iris while deliberately blurring the background crocuses beyond recognition, by setting an aperture of f4. The resulting colour reflects a detail of a painting by Picasso.
Nikon F9OX, 200mm macro lens, f4, Fujichrome Velvia film

KNICKER PINK (page 36)
Dahlia 'Figurine'
Dahlias, in bloom throughout the summer until the first frosts, are excellent for providing late colour in the border. This specimen, a water lily type, is reminiscent of a lotus flower.
Olympus OM2, 90mm macro lens, f22, Fujichrome Velvia film

***HEDDA GABLER*, CAMBRIDGE THEATRE 1970 (page 37)**
Hyacinthus 'Blue Magic'
Rain intensifies colour, increasing saturation and contributing sparkle to photographs. Certainly the case here where the resulting unusual colouring recalls the production of *Hedda Gabler* at the Cambridge Theatre, London, in the early seventies.
Olympus OM2, 90mm macro lens, f4, Fujichrome Velvia film

LARCH WOOD (page 38)
Melianthus major
The rich colouring of the melianthus, closely resembling a larch wood in spring, is achieved by the midday sun passing through the leaves towards the camera. To protect the lens from direct rays of light, a lens hood and sheet of card were used.
Olympus OM2, 90mm macro lens, f5.6, Fujichrome Velvia film

FIRELOCK (page 39)
Ranunculus asiaticus
To render everything pin-sharp, and to give a bee's eye view of the world, a macro lens and small aperture (f22) were used for this image. A sheet of white card placed close to the flower boosts the amount of natural daylight.
Olympus OM2, 90mm macro lens, f22, Fujichrome Velvia film

IN THE LIMELIGHT (page 40)
Anthemis tinctoria **'E C Buxton'**
With a background thrown out of focus, attention is directly drawn to this individual flower head which, personified, appears as a rather satisfied player taking a curtain call. A large aperture (f4) serves to isolate the subject from its surroundings.
Olympus OM2, 90mm macro lens, f4, Fujichrome Velvia film

HITCHENS *FLOWER COMPOSITION* (page 41)
Papaver somniferum
A shallow depth of field in the picture gives to this image an ethereal, contemplative quality. Strong winds necessitated a shutter speed of 1/500 second in order to eliminate any flower movement.
Olympus OM2, 75–210mm zoom lens, f4, Fujichrome Velvia film

FOOTLIGHT (page 42)
Papaver nudicaule
Pink and yellow combined are, at very least, provocative. The juxtaposition of these two colours appeared in a poppy growing in designer Keeyla Meadows' garden in San Francisco. The flower was picked out with a zoom lens while a fast shutter speed of 1/250 second froze for that moment the motion of the flower.
Olympus OM2, 75–210mm zoom lens, f8, Fujichrome Velvia film

AGAINST THE BLITZ (page 43)
Crocosmia **'Lady Hamilton'**
Early morning or, as here, sunset are ideal times to photograph hot-coloured plants when the warm glow of the sun saturates the colour. In this instance a late-flowering crocosmia appears as though shot against a city in flames.
Olympus OM2, 90mm macro lens, f4, Fujichrome Velvia film

SULPHUR POLYPORES (page 44)
Tulipa 'Professor Röntgen'
Nearing the end of their flowering period, these spectacular parrot tulips were shot in the Keukenhof Gardens in Holland in the soft light of early morning. The richness of their colour, and the detail of their texture, cause them to appear as a fungus in some woodland setting.
Pentax 67, 135mm macro lens, f32, Fujichrome Velvia film

SIXTIES SHADES (page 45)
Tulipa 'Fantasy'
Warm evening light bathes this tulip in an ethereal glow, the green flash on the undersides of the petals proving particularly attractive. Blue, out-of-focus pansies provide a suitable foil to the flower.
Olympus OM2, 90mm macro lens, f16, Fujichrome Velvia film

EDWARDIAN CORSAGE (page 47)
Verbascum nigrum
Autumn borders at The Royal Horticultural Society Garden at Wisley, Surrey, inspired this unusual image in which early flowering purple asters serve to show off the pale yellow flowers of the verbascum. A large aperture (f4) ensured a shallow depth of field.
Olympus OM2, 75–210mm zoom lens, f4, Fujichrome Velvia film

BALLROOM DANCER (page 49)
Camellia x *williamsii* 'Shocking Pink'
The isolation of pattern on a small scale, in this instance working with a 90mm macro lens, is endlessly fascinating. Here the image recalls not only the intensity and variation of colour in this early flowering camellia, but also the superb symmetry to be appreciated in the gradually unfurling petals which, in opening, convey a very real sense of rhythm and movement.
Olympus OM2, 90mm macro lens, f22, Fujichrome Velvia film

STARGAZER (page 51)
Ipomoea 'Heavenly Blue'
That a four-year-old should liken the flower of this *Ipomoea* cultivar to the Star of Bethlehem is easily imagined. In close up, the linear structure of the petal formation and the central disc, which appears to radiate its own light, are immediately suggestive of the night sky. Coupled with this is the ethereal quality of the subject, a beauty captured in soft, overcast light.
Olympus OM2, 90mm macro lens with extension tube, f16, Fujichrome Velvia film

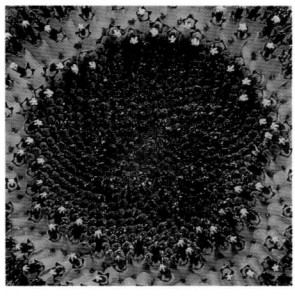

INCA EMPIRE (page 53)
Helianthus annuus 'Titan'
Sunflowers make for bold statements which translate into dramatic pictures. Possibly more than any other flower, it is their exciting and complex structure, supported by unflinching colour, which offers such a wealth of photographic opportunity. Seemingly house-high, this particular specimen required a step ladder, in addition to a long-legged tripod, to capture it on film.
Olympus OM2, 90mm macro lens, f22, Fujichrome Velvia film

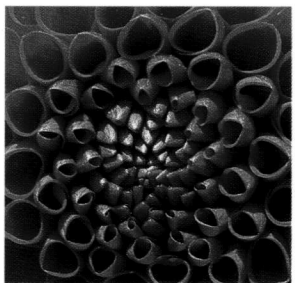

COMMUNION AT CHARTRES (page 54)
Dahlia 'Long's Red Admiral'
Dahlias have in recent years been considered by many to be unfashionable. Enjoying a current revival in popularity, their controlled form and bold colours make them ideal candidates for late summer and autumn borders. 'Long's Red Admiral' possesses such perfect patterning that the image was believed by one art director to have been generated by computer.
Olympus OM2, 90mm macro lens, f22, Fujichrome Velvia film

PARTIAL ECLIPSE (page 55)
Helianthus annuus 'Titan'
Where previously the central disc florets of the sunflower were the centre of attention (page 53), here the emphasis alters to concentrate on the outer petals with their uniform pattern serving to define a regular shape. Interestingly, the visual link between this image and the view of Magdalen Bridge explores the ways in which the manmade world draws upon and is indebted to that of nature.
Olympus OM2, 90mm macro lens, f22, Fujichrome Velvia film

MAGDALEN MOON (page 55)
Magdalen Bridge from Oxford Botanic Garden
Too often what appears obvious is disregarded. Such was the case with this view of Magdalen Bridge, thought a subject of no particular interest by a group of rain-soaked students. Seen from a different angle, in this instance from the footpath which runs beside the River Cherwell, the water, the bridge and the tethered boats take on a new, totally different, identity.
Olympus OM2, 75–210mm zoom lens, f11, Fujichrome Velvia film

CATHERINE WHEEL ON WATERED SILK (page 56)
Helleborus orientalis
Photographing the hanging heads of the late winter-flowering hellebores can be problematical. To capture their intriguing down-turned faces often involves a stick to act as a prop. This specimen was growing on a bank and fortunately required no such staking.
Olympus OM2, 90mm macro lens, f22, Fujichrome Velvia film

THE THIN BLUE LINE (page 57)
Cabbages and chard, Château de Villandry, France
Situated in the Loire Valley, the spectacular potager at the Château de Villandry is in itself a tour de force of conceit, design and pattern. Extending to more than an acre in size, the intricately contrived, box-edged borders house upwards of 60,000 vegetable plants annually. Viewed from the terraces above, this small section is captured with the aid of a zoom lens, utilised to highlight the contrast of colour, texture and form.
Olympus OM2, 75–210mm zoom lens, f32, Fujichrome Velvia film

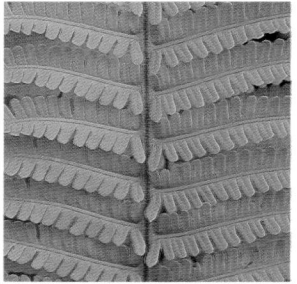

GREEN SPINE CHILLER (page 58)
Matteuccia struthiopteris
Much of the appeal of the ostrich fern lies in the disciplined structure of its apple-green fronds which emanate from a single stem in almost skeletal manner. Seen in detail here, the well-defined image was shot on an uninviting, damp and overcast morning, the weather assisting in drawing out the intensity of the subject.
Olympus OM2, 90mm macro lens, f22, Fujichrome Velvia film

LOVE HEARTS (page 59)
The Garden of Love, Château de Villandry, France
The Jardin d'Amour with its colourful box-edged borders is as remarkable as it is renowned. A zoom lens was employed to crop into the strong pattern formed by the shape of the hedges.
Olympus OM2, 75–210mm zoom lens, f32, Fujichrome Velvia film

PLOUGHED PINE (page 60)
Pinus pinea
This wonderful specimen is to be seen at Kew Gardens in London. Early morning sunlight rakes across the surface of the tree, emphasising the three-dimensional quality of the bark. An image such as this one recalls Landsat pictures of mountain regions, familiar to all students of physical geography.
Olympus OM2, 75–210mm zoom lens, f32, Fujichrome Velvia film

TWO DIRECTIONAL (page 61)
Prunus serrula
The strength of this image lies in its very simplicity. Arrow-like markings, coming from both left and right, appear in relief against the deep mahogany of the tree's main trunk. Evening sunlight adds further depth.
Olympus OM2, 90mm macro lens, f22, Fujichrome Velvia film

DAY-GLO (page 62)
Gazania **'Sunset Jane'**
Of interest are the extravagant markings of these sun-loving flowers which display a quality of luminosity, giving the appearance of being visible in the dark. To this end 'Day-Glo' seems a very appropriate title.
Olympus OM2, 90mm macro lens, f22, Fujichrome Velvia film

WOOD SHAVINGS (page 63)
Ranunculus asiaticus
The work of bird and animal photographers, such as Frans Lanting and Laurie Campbell, are always of interest. A close up of a bird's plumage by Lanting inspired this image, although a bird is replaced with a ranunculus, plumage with petals.
Olympus OM2, 90mm macro lens, f22, Fujichrome Velvia film

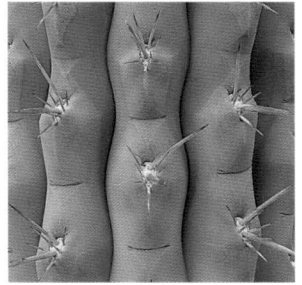

BODY PIERCING (page 64)
Browningia hartlingianus
Cacti, such as this *Browningia hartlingianus* and *Pachycereus pringlei* (page 66), rely on spines to fend off predators and thus ensure survival. Their leaves, not requiring a high chlorophyll content, often appear grey-blue.
Olympus OM2, 90mm macro lens, f22, Fujichrome Velvia film

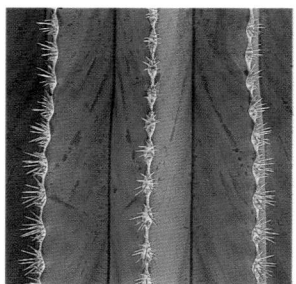

DESERT HIGHWAY (page 66)
Pachycereus pringlei
Something of the austere, arid nature of the desert is suggested in this cactus with its prickles and hairs. As a subject it is vastly different from many of the softer, more gentle plants to be found in gardens throughout the world.
Olympus OM2, 90mm macro lens, f22, Fujichrome Velvia film

A FANFARE OF PIPES (page 67)
Chrysanthemum 'Louisa'
Close cropping resulted in this image of a section of chrysanthemum with its suggestion of organ pipes. In content it also resembles the oars of rowing boats. Both possess a similar thrusting quality.
Olympus OM2, 90mm macro lens, f22, Fujichrome Velvia film

GORGEOUS GREEN TAFFETA (pages 68–9)
Zantedeschia aethiopica
Generally it is the arch-like, white spathes of the zantedeschia that appeal to the photographer. Less usual is a depiction of the mini 'arrowhead' evident at the base of the leaves. Using the rule of thirds, the image was framed so that the 'arrowhead' lay on one of the 'points of power'.
Olympus OM2, 90mm macro lens, f16, Fujichrome Velvia film

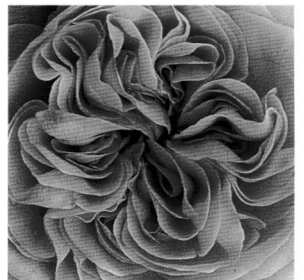

PUCKERED PINK SATIN (page 71)
Rosa 'Gertrude Jekyll'
The way in which the centre of this rose appears to be gathered in makes for the subject's interest. Taken in overcast light with a small aperture, the definition becomes all the more acute.
Olympus OM2, 90mm macro lens, f22, Fujichrome Velvia film

BODY ARMOUR (pages 72–3)
Agave parryii, **Huntington Botanical Garden, Los Angeles**
Who could resist this huge agave growing among the 2,500 different species of plants to be found in the desert garden of The Huntington Botanical Garden in Los Angeles? Its succulent, fleshy leaves have a fearsome quality making the title 'Body Armour' singularly appropriate.
Olympus OM2, 75–210mm zoom lens, f32, Fujichrome Velvia film

SUPER NOVA (pages 74–5)
Echium wildpretii
Like a star exploding in space, the silver-green leaves of this echium at the Chelsea Physic Garden in London spray out from the plant's heart. To emphasise the length of the leaves, the middle of the plant is deliberately placed off-centre.
Olympus OM2, 50mm standard lens, f16, Fujichrome Velvia film

GHOSTLY CONVOY (pages 76–7)
Betula utilis
Although the appearance of the bark suggests that it has been scored several times with a sharp knife, this is in fact a natural occurrence. It is this effect, of course, which makes for the interest, as does the chalky colour of the wood.
Olympus OM2, 90mm macro lens, f22, Fujichrome Velvia film

ICE-CAPPED MAIDENS (page 78)
Statues for sale at Sprivers Garden, Kent
Photographing in snow is always exciting. On this occasion, to find the snow meant a November drive of over a hundred miles to this architectural garden in Kent with its wealth of urns and statues. Appealing above all else were these stone heads, lined up in readiness for sale to the public.
Olympus OM2, 75–210mm zoom lens, f22, Fujichrome Velvia film

ONE STEP AHEAD OF THE REST (page 79)
Deities by Patricia Volk
Such artistry is present in the placement of these sculptures which appear to be randomly distributed across the ground. As a close study of the image reveals, this is far from the case. The Hannah Peschar Sculpture Gallery in Surrey remains among the very best of places in England to view contemporary sculpture.
Olympus OM2, 50mm standard lens, f16, Fujichrome Velvia film

IN MOURNING (page 81)
Aquilegia vulgaris
One of the principal concerns in photographing flowers is to ensure that an individual subject has character and form, something that will set it aside from others. On a cold, damp summer morning this delicate, beautifully coloured columbine seemed to have everything, and more besides.
Olympus OM2, 90mm macro lens, f22, Fujichrome Velvia film

LADIES DAY AT ASCOT (page 83)
Magnolia campbellii 'Charles Raffill'
Taking up to twelve years to flower, this magnolia, when it does, is certainly worth the wait as candyfloss-pink petals curl open suggestively to reveal peachy-pink stamens. A deep blue sky becomes the perfect backdrop to this majestic specimen, photographed at flowering time in the Chelsea Physic Garden, London, one March.
Olympus OM2, 90mm macro lens, f2.8, Fujichrome Velvia film

TURBO JET (page 85)
Papaver orientale 'Patty's Plum'
Of all the oriental poppies, this must be one of the most desirable on account of the richness of its colouring. Although fleetingly in flower, it remains an excellent choice for the herbaceous border. In this image the interior of the flower makes an association with a turbo jet engine.
Olympus OM2, 90mm macro lens, f22, Fujichrome Velvia film

EMBRYO (page 86)
Nectaroscordum siculum
As this sequence of images illustrates, *Nectaroscordum siculum*, a bulbous plant related to the allium, is fascinating at every stage of its development from bud to seedhead. Particularly attractive are the bell-shaped, pale green flowers which, flushed with light plum, gently fade to brown before inverting their heads skywards.
Olympus OM2, 90mm macro lens, f4, Fujichrome Velvia film

BIRTH (page 86)
Nectaroscordum siculum
See description above.
Olympus OM2, 90mm macro lens, f4, Fujichrome Velvia film

INFANCY (page 86)
Nectaroscordum siculum
See description above.
Olympus OM2, 90mm macro lens, f4, Fujichrome Velvia film

COMING OF AGE (page 87)
Nectaroscordum siculum
See description above.
Olympus OM2, 90mm macro lens, f11, Fujichrome Velvia film

PUNK (page 88)
Clematis orientalis
As with so many clematis, the flowers of *Clematis orientalis* are followed in autumn and through into winter by creamy brown 'wigs'. These silky, feathery seedheads are delightful to touch and appear quite sensuous when they are misted over with the morning's dewdrops. Here the image is suggestive of the rather way-out hair style favoured by the young of some years ago.
Olympus OM2, 90mm macro lens, f4, Fujichrome Velvia film

WAX TAPERS (page 89)
Garrya elliptica
Captured here are the long, tapering, silvery catkins of the winter garrya. Starting off green in late summer, they gradually increase in length, changing colour as they do so. A mature specimen becomes one of the delights of the out-of-season garden.
Olympus OM2, 75–210mm zoom lens, f8, Fujichrome Velvia film

ICED MOPHEADS (page 90)
Euphorbia characias subsp. *wulfenii*
The shrubby spurges of the Mediterranean regions are excellent architectural plants for the border, their tall inflorescences providing strong form throughout the year. Here, chilled by the cold of winter, they resemble mopheads awaiting use.
Olympus OM2, 50mm standard lens, f16, Fujichrome Velvia film

CRYSTALLISED DAISIES (page 91)
Euphorbia x *martinii*
To obtain a crisp, pin-sharp image of these euphorbia heads, frozen in time at The Royal Horticultural Society Garden at Wisley, Surrey, a macro lens was set with the smallest aperture possible (f22). To avoid camera shake it was mounted on a sturdy tripod. The result: a series of daisy-like forms.
Olympus OM2, 90mm macro lens, f22, Fujichrome Velvia film

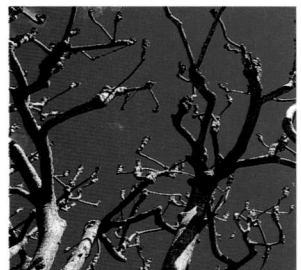

FILIGREE (page 92)
Plane trees, Lake Como, Italy
These magnificent trees are to be found in the garden of the Villa del Balbianello on Lake Como in northern Italy. Each year they are pruned into a series of wonderful, candelabra shapes. A wide-angle lens and low viewpoint combine to provide a strong contrast between the intense blue of the sky and the silver trunks of the plane trees.
Olympus OM2, 21mm wide-angle lens, f11, Fujichrome Velvia film

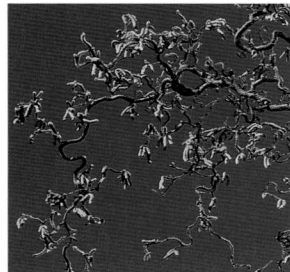

COSTUME JEWELLERY (page 93)
Corylus avellana 'Contorta'
Popularly known as the corkscrew hazel, this rather strange tree, prized for its Quasimodo-like habit, makes for an unusual and interesting subject. A low viewpoint and wide-angle lens, as in the previous image of plane trees, is used to set the twisted branches, with their dangling catkins, against the blue of a winter sky.
Olympus OM2, 28mm wide-angle lens, f11, Fujichrome Velvia film

EASTERN SWEETMEATS (page 94)
Lupinus 'Paddington Bear'
The structure of the lupin becomes the focus of this image. By concentrating on a section of the flower, rather than considering it as a whole, there is a dramatic change of emphasis. Here the individual florets, perhaps because of their bold colour and shape, come to resemble the delicious sweets obtainable in the Far East.
Olympus OM2, 90mm macro lens, f22, Fujichrome Velvia film

PRIZE BUNCH (page 95)
Kniphofia triangularis
Seen close up, the flower of the poker takes on the appearance of, say, a bunch of carrots placed on display and waiting to take away First Prize at the local garden show. Two extension tubes on the macro lens were combined with an aperture of f22 in order to obtain maximum depth of field.
Olympus OM2, 90mm macro lens with 44mm of extension tubes, f22, Fujichrome Velvia film

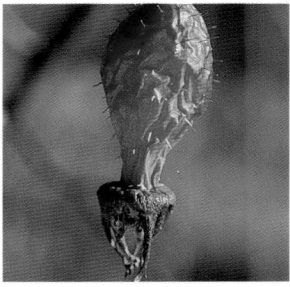

SEALING WAX (page 96)
Rosa moyesii 'Geranium'
An ideal shrub for the smaller garden, *Rosa moyesii* 'Geranium' not only has flowers of blood-red but these are followed by autumnal hips, looking as here like globular drops of sealing wax. This specimen was growing alongside a small pool in the garden of Dolwen in Wales.
Olympus OM2, 90mm macro lens, f8, Fujichrome Velvia film

BUTTERFLY NUT ATTIRED (page 97)
Parrotia persica
The Persian ironwood tree is a member of the witch hazel family. In late winter it produces strange, vivid red flowers. Beginning as a tight cluster of small deep orange fingers, the stamens break out from round, brown bracts. In this image the smooth backdrop is, in fact, branches from the tree itself, blown out of focus.
Olympus OM2, 90mm macro lens with 44mm of extension tubes, f22, Fujichrome Velvia film

TOMATO ON THE VINE (page 99)
Papaver orientale
Going against the traditional approach to plant portraiture, this oriental poppy was shot from behind. Bright light on an otherwise overcast day, combined with Fujichrome Velvia film and a small aperture, ensured that every detail of the flower petals was clearly reproduced.
Olympus OM2, 90mm macro lens, f22, Fujichrome Velvia film

WINDSOCKS (page 100)
Tropaeolum tricolorum
The flowers of this perennial nasturtium really do resemble gaily coloured windsocks fluttering happily in a gentle breeze. By using a large aperture on the macro lens, it was possible to throw the green background out of focus, thus concentrating attention on the strange form of the flowers themselves.
Olympus OM2, 90mm macro lens with 31mm extension tube, f8, Fujichrome Velvia film

INFLIGHT FUELLING (page 101)
Salvia fulgens
Indigenous to Mexico where it is a forest dweller, *Salvia fulgens* is capable of reaching in excess of 1m (3ft) in height. A side-on perspective of this deep scarlet, velvet-furry salvia clearly illustrates its two 'lips' and forms the connection between it and the title, 'Inflight Fuelling'.
Olympus OM2, 90mm macro lens, f5.6, Fujichrome Velvia film

CONSTRUCTION KIT (page 102)
Cornus sanguinea 'Winter Flame'
Cornus, or dogwoods, are among the most spectacular of all shrubs for winter stem colour. 'Winter Flame' is no exception to this, with its striking tones of pink-red. In the image, the arrangement of branches takes on the appearance of a three-dimensional, brightly painted construction kit.
Olympus OM2, 90mm macro lens, f4, Fujichrome Velvia film

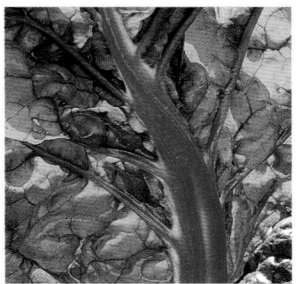

AORTA (page 103)
Ruby chard
Backlight on the leaf of this ruby chard creates a translucent quality which reveals the curved nature of the blood-red stem and the crumpled form of the leaf. It does indeed resemble the great artery issuing from the left ventricle of the heart.
Olympus OM2, 75–210mm zoom lens, f16, Fujichrome Velvia film

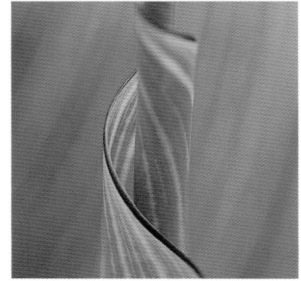

HELTER SKELTER (page 104)
Canna 'Striata'
Spotted during a lesson being given to a group of students on the use of a macro lens, this canna leaf unfurling from within another, larger leaf became a point of interest. The strong impression of movement and tension was obtained by focusing on the edge of the 'helter skelter' and using a shallow depth of field to throw the background leaf out of focus.
Olympus OM2, 90mm macro lens, f4, Fujichrome Velvia film

BLOOD MOLECULES (page 105)
Hippeastrum
This picture clearly demonstrates just how little depth of field it is possible to achieve when taking an extreme close up with macro lens and extension tubes. Even with the smallest aperture possible, f22, only the tiny pollen-dusted stamens are in sharp focus.
Olympus OM2, 90mm macro lens with 44mm of extension tubes, f22, Fujichrome Velvia film

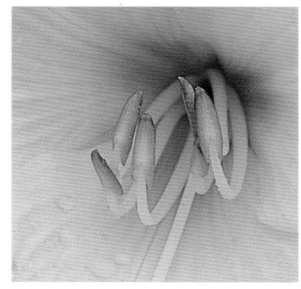

SHERBERT DIP (page 106)
Hemerocallis 'Perennial Pleasure'
The natural daylight entering the throat of this daylily proved too weak to show up the internal structure of the flower. To counter this, a white reflector was held just beneath the surface so that the ambient daylight bounced back to boost the overall light level. As a matter of course, reflectors are used in preference to flash as the results may be viewed through the lens.
Olympus OM2, 90mm macro lens, f22, Fujichrome Velvia film

FURLED PARASOL (page 107)
Muscari armeniacum
The Keukenhof Gardens in Holland are famous for their tulip plantings but other spring bulbs, such as muscari, are widely used as well. In this picture yellow pansies, placed out of focus, provide a complementary backdrop to the blue of the grape hyacinth. The whole makes for a joyous, summery scene.
Olympus OM2, 90mm macro lens, f2.8, Fujichrome Velvia film

RIPE FRUIT (page 108)
Iris foetidissima
Although rather dull when in flower, *Iris foetidissima* performs better in the autumn when the seedheads split to reveal bright orange berries, fitting snugly like peas in their pod or, as the title suggests, like over-ripe fruit. Whatever, the resulting picture is both startling and arresting.
Olympus OM2, 90mm macro lens, f16, Fujichrome Velvia film

CLASSICAL URN AT SUNSET (page 109)
Tulipa 'Ballerina'
The underlying thought behind this image was to recreate the sensation of looking at the urn-shaped tulip through the border at ground level. An aperture of f8 was used to give precision to the tulip, at the same time throwing other flowers and the surrounding foliage completely out of focus.
Olympus OM2, 90mm macro lens, f8, Fujichrome Velvia film

SURREALISM (page 111)
Frosted ruby chard
Some of the most dramatic effects are achieved at first light. For the garden photographer this often involves starting work at an impossibly early hour to be on location at the right time to secure a shot. This image was taken early in the morning on a November day at The Royal Horticultural Society Garden at Wisley in Surrey.
Olympus OM2, 90mm macro lens, f22, Fujichrome Velvia film

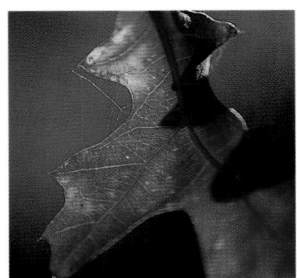

MOLTEN ORE (page 113)
Red oak leaf
Caught by a gentle breeze, this oak leaf refused to remain still. To freeze its movement, a shutter speed of 1/500 second was selected. To achieve this meant sacrificing depth of field by using a large aperture of f4 on a zoom lens.
Olympus OM2, 75–210mm zoom lens, f4, Fujichrome Velvia film

CHINESE LACQUER (page 115)
Acer cappadocicum 'Rubrum'
Here the area of deep shade behind the leaves of the acer forms a velvety, black background which serves to emphasise the brilliance of the principal subject matter. The title, 'Chinese Lacquer', is appropriate for its suggestion of bright light and vibrant colour.
Olympus OM2, 75–210mm zoom lens, f32, Fujichrome Velvia film

IMPRESSIONISM (page 116–7)
Tulips, Gardens of Mainau, Lake Constance
A little-known garden situated on an island on Lake Constance. In springtime, great drifts of tulips cover the hillsides which fall to the water's edge, the whole resembling a canvas by an impressionist painter. A truly dazzling picture. This is a garden which deserves to be more widely appreciated.
Olympus OM2, 75–210mm zoom lens, f32, Fujichrome Velvia film

***HOW GREEN WAS MY VALLEY* (page 118)**
Dolwen, Powys, Wales
A totally magical garden of streams and natural plantings, carved from a Welsh hillside. To capture this light-filled moment of sunrise bursting over a nearby slope, involved a drive of over 200 miles. The end result is an image which conveys the total beauty, peace and solitude of this isolated valley.
Bronica SQA 6x6, 80mm standard lens, f22, Fujichrome Velvia film

UPLIGHTER (page 119)
Anthemis tinctoria 'E C Buxton'
The emphasis in this image is directed towards the flower bloom which, radiating light, appears to float in space. The reason for this is the very shallow depth of field in the picture which has taken the stem completely out of focus.
Olympus OM2, 90mm macro lens, f2.5, Fujichrome Velvia film

COLD CHARMIAN (page 120)
Sculpture by Helen Sinclair, The Arrow Cottage Garden, Herefordshire
In summer a profusion of plants tends to overshadow this sculpture, at times masking it almost entirely. Not so in winter when, coated with hoar frost and backlit with pale sunlight, the piece takes centre stage. Possibly it is out of season that garden sculptures, unrivalled, come into their own.
Bronica SQA 6x6, 80mm standard lens, f22, Fujichrome Velvia film

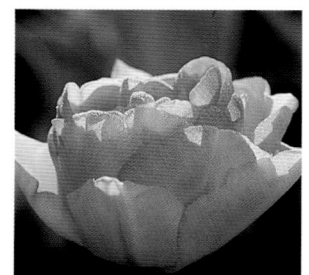

DRESDEN DETAIL (page 121)
Tulipa 'Angélique'
Taken in the rose garden at Coton Manor in Northamptonshire on a spring morning when the light was near electric, this tulip possesses all the qualities of a piece of fine porcelain. The intense white, appearing as icing sugar, is of course the early morning dew.
Olympus OM2, 90mm macro lens, f8, Fujichrome Velvia film

SPARKLING WINE (page 122)
Camellia sasanqua 'Sparkling Burgundy'
An early flowering camellia, often in bloom in England during the late winter. When this image was shot, most of the flowers had fallen so the picture was taken from above, the fallen petals employed to create a harmonious background to the main subject.
Olympus OM2, 50mm standard lens, f8, Fujichrome Velvia film

PINK PLASTIC (page 123)
Echinacea purpurea 'Rubinstern'
The intensity of the light in this image gives the petals of the coneflower a somewhat artificial quality so that the unusual shade of pink appears as moulded plastic. The upright and controlled form of this attractive herbaceous perennial makes it an ideal photographic subject.
Olympus OM2, 90mm macro lens, f11, Fujichrome Velvia film

A WINTER'S TALE **(page 125)**
Chiswick House, London
The handsome eighteenth-century gardens of Chiswick House were created from 1716 and later extended by William Kent to complement the Palladian villa built by the first Lord Burlington in 1729. In winter, when many gardens have lost their charm, the strong structure of trees, hedges and ornament at Chiswick come into their own.
Bronica SQA 6x6, 80mm standard lens, f22, Fujichrome Velvia film

SILENT WITNESS (page 126)
Statue of Venus, Rousham Landscape Garden, Oxfordshire
Alexander Pope described Rousham as 'the prettiest place for waterfalls, jetts, ponds, inclosed with beautiful scenes of green and hanging wood, that I ever saw'. Designed by William Kent in 1738, these landscape grounds seem frozen in time. Here the rising sun illuminates one of many statues.
Bronica SQA 6x6, 50mm wide-angle lens, f16, Fujichrome Velvia film

CHILLED HISTORY (page 127)
Hatfield House, Hertfordshire
Originally laid out in the early seventeenth century by Robert Cecil and planted by John Tradescant the Elder, the gardens at Hatfield House have in recent years undergone considerable restoration and transformation. This picture, taken shortly after dawn on a cold, misty November morning, captures completely the unique atmosphere and spirit of Hatfield.
Olympus OM2, 75–210mm zoom lens, f16, Fujichrome Velvia film

FAIRY LANTERNS (page 128)
Leucojum aestivum **'Gravetye Giant'**
Although a close relative of the snowdrop, the summer snowflake is taller in stature, up to a surprising 1m (3ft) in some cases, and their six petals are of equal rather than different lengths. The apparent delicacy of their form, as well as their whiteness, make the title 'Fairy Lanterns' more than appropriate.
Olympus OM2, 90mm macro lens, f8, Fujichrome Velvia film

ART NOUVEAU (page 129)
Galanthus **'Atkinsii'**
Beautifully shaped, the flower head of the snowdrop is in reality, on account of its small size, a difficult subject to photograph. This image required the use of macro lens, extension tubes and, of course, a tripod.
Olympus OM2, 90mm macro lens with 31mm extension tube, f2.8, Fujichrome Velvia film

SPRING GALAXY (page 130)
Crocus tomasinianus
Known affectionately as 'tommies', these cheerful lavender bulbs are usually the earliest of the crocuses to appear, opening wide when warmed by the sun. Together with snowdrops, *Galanthus nivalis*, and butter-yellow winter aconites, *Eranthis hyemalis*, they are true heralds of spring.
Bronica SQA 6x6, 80mm standard lens, f22, Fujichrome Velvia film

BLOWN GLASS (page 131)
Allium sphaerocephalon
Bright early morning backlight, highlights the tightly folded bud of this allium, just hours before it bursts from its protective sheath. In its present form it bears a marked similarity to blown glass, sharing a translucency and fragility.
Olympus OM2, 90mm macro lens, f8, Fujichrome Velvia film

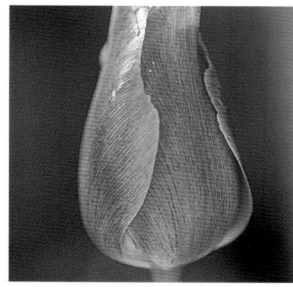

QUIETISM (page 132)
Tulipa 'Don Quichotte'
With the flower head in open shade, a white reflector was employed in this situation to bounce some natural daylight on to this tulip. Caught before the tulip opened fully, the additional light serves to give an ethereal quality to the subject.
Olympus OM2, 90mm macro lens, f11, Fujichrome Velvia film

LAST OF SUMMER (page 133)
Rosa 'Rosemary Rose'
Such a rose as this one, encrusted in frost, is magical, a reminder of a summer long gone. Speed is of the essence at times like this, for before too long, the day's temperature will have lifted and the moment will be lost and the subject gone forever.
Olympus OM2, 90mm macro lens, f16, Fujichrome Velvia film

AT HOME WITH MISS HAVISHAM (page 134)
Cobweb, Ridley's Cheer, Wiltshire
Laden with moisture, this cobweb becomes an interesting and atmospheric subject for a picture. To achieve the effect it was necessary to ensure that the dawn light was directed straight through the cobweb towards the camera. Care was taken to screen the lens with a lens hood and a piece of black card.
Olympus OM2, 75–210mm zoom lens, f5.6, Fujichrome Velvia film

FLICKERING FLAME (page 135)
Stipa gigantea
This gigantic perennial grass originates in the Iberian Peninsula and North Africa. The flowers start off purplish-green in colour, but as summer turns to autumn the dangling anthers turn to burnished gold. Seen in close up, and backlit by a glowing evening light, the anthers take on the appearance of flames.
Olympus OM2, 90mm macro lens, f2.8, Fujichrome Velvia film

DIPPED IN SUGAR (page 137)
Astrantia major 'Hadspen Blood'
Superb colour and good form ensure that this perennial masterwort is always sought after. Here, sparkling with dew drops, as though some confection dipped in sugar, this stem is shown to good effect when caught in the light of early morning.
Olympus OM2, 90mm macro lens, f4, Fujichrome Velvia film

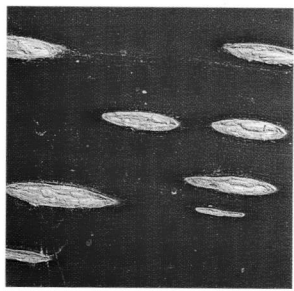

PUNCTURED PLASTIC (page 139)
Prunus serrula
A comparison of this image with the similar one on page 61 illustrates that in nature, seldom is anything the same. Although both pictures show the bark of *Prunus serrula*, they are in essence completely different.
Olympus OM2, 90mm macro lens, f16, Fujichrome Velvia film

PAPER LANTERNS (page 141)
Fritillaria imperialis **'Orange Perfection'**
The large, deep orange bell-shaped flowers of the crown imperial for all the world resemble the paper lanterns that feature so prominently in the parades to celebrate Chinese New Year. Here they make for a striking and tactile image.
Olympus OM2, 90mm macro lens, f16, Fujichrome Velvia film

MELLOW FRUITFULNESS (page 143)
Pumpkin
Photographed from above, the tough, leathery surface of this pumpkin is revealed. The inclusion of a part of the stem contributes scale and, importantly, provides a textural contrast to the picture.
Olympus OM2, 90mm macro lens, f16, Fujichrome Velvia film

SCORCHED EARTH (page 144)
Rodgersia pinnata **'Elegans'**
Backlighting is used here to highlight the three-dimensional quality of the leaf, creating an unusual and thought-provoking effect. No longer a single leaf, it becomes something much larger, more dreadful, terrifying even.
Olympus OM2, 90mm macro lens, f8, Fujichrome Velvia film

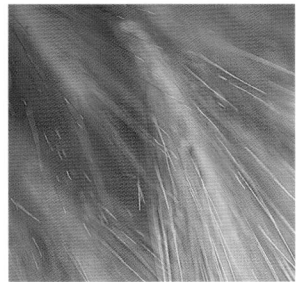

FIBRE OPTICS (page 145)
Hordeum jubatum
The soft, silky awns of this attractive grass are revealed in a delicate portrait shot in a moment of brightness on an otherwise overcast morning. Grasses like this one increasingly play an important part in the new perennial borders of Europe and America's foremost garden designers.
Olympus OM2, 90mm macro lens, f4, Fujichrome Velvia film

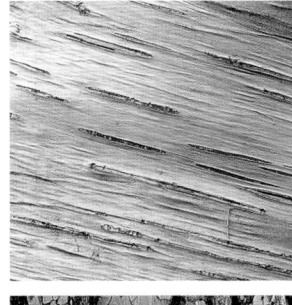

CHARCOAL AND SEPIA WASH (page 146)
Betula utilis
Most striking about all of the birches is the textural quality of their peeling bark. On this occasion the image centres on a section of trunk where successive layers of bark are coloured orange-brown and copper, overlaid with a grey-pink bloom.
Olympus OM2, 90mm macro lens, f11, Fujichrome Velvia film

SHALE STRATUM (page 147)
Pinus nigra **subsp.** *maritima*
Overwhelming in height, this specimen of *Pinus nigra* subsp. *maritima* is one of several to be found in Kew Gardens, London. The thickness of the trunk allowed for one section to be detailed, the result suggestive of a layer of the earth's crust.
Olympus OM2, 50mm standard lens, f16, Fujichrome Velvia film

POMPON (pages 148–9)
Flower of globe artichoke
So impressive is the stature of the globe artichoke, that it is easy to overlook the detail of the thistle-like, mauve-purple flower heads. Caught here is a close-up of the flower, seen by the camera to be a tuft of ribbon on hat or maybe shoe.
Olympus OM2, 90mm macro lens with 13mm extension tube, f22, Fujichrome Velvia film

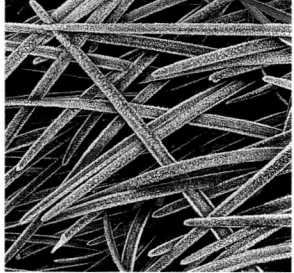

SABRES RATTLING (page 151)
Ophiopogon planiscapus 'Nigrescens'
Contrary to popular belief, this image was in fact taken on colour film and not in black and white. The key to its powerful composition is the arrow-like blade of the grass that cuts diagonally through the image to divide the picture into two matching triangles.
Olympus OM2, 90mm macro lens, f22, Fujichrome Velvia film

SAVOY AT MIDNIGHT (pages 152–3)
Frosted cabbage
All cabbages become magical when dusted with frost, and they are among the favourite subjects to photograph in the winter kitchen garden. Here the intense cold, conveyed in the blue of the image, serves to highlight the corrugated texture of the tired leaves.
Olympus OM2, 90mm macro lens, f22, Fujichrome Velvia film

EXOTIC PLUMAGE (pages 154–5)
Canna 'Striata'
The showy cannas, from the warmer parts of North and South America, add a touch of the tropics to any garden. Grown as much for its ornamental foliage as for its colourful, orchid-like flowers, *Canna* 'Striata' has some of the most striking leaves of all. Here backlighting creates a translucent quality which shows off exceptional variegation.
Olympus OM2, 50mm standard lens, f8, Fujichrome Velvia film

SOAPY SPINES (pages 156–7)
Aloe polyphylla
An extreme close-up of this plant reveals a range of pointed green peaks. The sharpness of the image, present throughout the composition, is brought about with the use of the smallest possible aperture on a 90mm macro lens.
Olympus OM2, 90mm macro lens, f22, Fujichrome Velvia film

PLEATED VELOURS (page 158)
Philodendron melanochrysum
Much of the attraction of this robust climber lies in its lengthy, heart-shaped, olive-green leaves. In this image, the focus is on one half of a single leaf to create an unusual, abstract picture which is suggestive of rich and plentiful curtaining velvet.
Olympus OM2, 50mm standard lens, f22, Fujichrome Velvia film

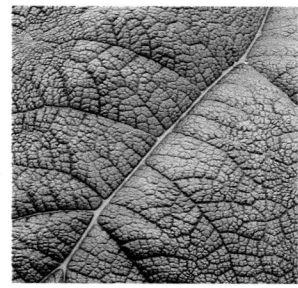

ELEPHANT HIDE (page 159)
Gunnera manicata
Children adore to shelter under the giant, spreading leaves of this huge, ornamental foliage plant during summer rainstorms. The thick, leathery leaves are almost brittle in texture, in winter closely resembling the hide of an elephant when, in decay, they take on a grey-brown appearance.
Olympus OM2, 75–210mm zoom lens, f32, Fujichrome Velvia film

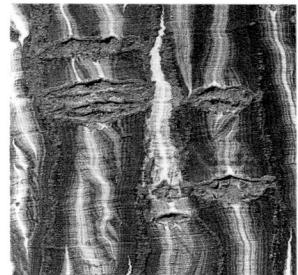

COUNTRY HOUSE CURTAINS (page 160)
Acer capillipes
As well as conveying something of the texture and quality of much used, somewhat worn but nonetheless favourite curtains, this image invites close inspection to reveal, concealed among the drapes, the face of the Green Man. As if this were not enough, further examination will reward with the outline of two circus acrobats.
Olympus OM2, 90mm macro lens, f11, Fujichrome Velvia film

PINCUSHION (page 161)
Opuntia pycnantha
To photograph this tiny section of *Opuntia pycnantha* required the use of a macro lens and two extension tubes. These push the lens further away from the camera body, enabling the lens to focus even closer. The resulting image could well be that of a pincushion.
Olympus OM2, 90mm macro lens with 44mm of extension tubes, f22, Fujichrome Velvia film

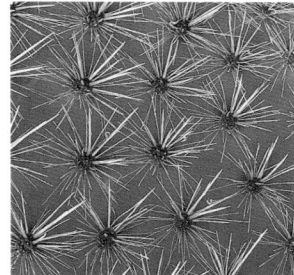

LIBERTY PRINT (pages 162–3)
Cephalocereus senilis
A further extreme close up, on this occasion taken in a cactus garden on Lanzarote in the Canary Islands. The fine needles on this plant, repeated all over the surface, could well belong on a pattern of material of the kind popular in late Victorian and Edwardian times.
Olympus OM2, 90mm macro lens, f16, Fujichrome Velvia film

SKIN DISEASE (page 164)
Ruby chard
The deeply folded texture of this ruby chard leaf is graphically illustrated in this picture. Indeed, the image has somewhat surprisingly unpleasant over-tones. Compare this with the portrayal of the same plant shown on page 171. There it is possible to note a complete transformation in terms of both texture and colour.
Olympus OM2, 90mm macro lens, f11, Fujichrome Velvia film

ARTERIAL BRUISING (page 165)
Rheum palmatum
A heavy rainstorm had battered the impressive leaves of this ornamental rhubarb, with the result that they had turned, as if in defence, to reveal their rich, plum undersides.
Olympus OM2, 90mm macro lens, f22, Fujichrome Velvia film

CARTIER BROOCH (page 167)
Ornamental cabbage
There is something remarkably tactile about the heavily frosted leaves of this ornamental cabbage. Intense cold has highlighted the frilled edges of each leaf, intensifying the pink and purple colouration, giving the whole a jewel-like quality, elevating it well beyond its garden setting.
Olympus OM2, 90mm macro lens, f22, Fujichrome Velvia film

SPOTLIGHT ON SATIN (page 168)
Alcea rosea 'Nigra'
The satin quality of the petals of this hollyhock, photographed at Hadspen Garden in Somerset, make a bold and dramatic statement. The golden centre of the flower is placed to the top right of the composition in order to draw attention to the veining of the petals.
Olympus OM2, 90mm macro lens with 13mm extension tube, f22, Fujichrome Velvia film

BOLT OF SILK (page 171)
Ruby chard
Mark Rothko (1903–1970), the Abstract Expressionist artist, wished for his paintings to immerse the viewer in a total colour experience. The intention here is similar. The image is designed principally to explore the texture of the chard, but also to encourage an appreciation of colour and form.
Olympus OM2, 90mm macro lens with 44mm of extension tubes, f22, Fujichrome Velvia film

ACKNOWLEDGEMENTS

I would like to thank the following people who have made this book possible. My wife, Jane, for her faith in the project and her management of the whole *New Shoots* brand. Lance Hattatt for his superb text and eye for design, and his wife Jane who has been a great supporter of the book; Joanna Smith for her dedication to the design and editing of the book; all the garden owners and sculptors whose work appears in the book; Sandra and Nori Pope who opened my eyes to the beauty within a leaf and flower; and Jamie Compton for checking the nomenclature of the plants. Finally, Roger Multon at Supreme Publishing Services, and Harry Ricketts and Grant Bradford at Fountain Press, for their guidance on all matters relating to production and printing.